JAHB: The Inviting End

Mike Spiritfair Marty

Get a JAHB, LLC: Milwaukee

Bibliographic Data

©2006 Michael Spiritfair Marty (Chapters 9-12)
      (Completion date: April 21, 2006)

All rights reserved. No part of this artistic expression may be used or reproduced in any manner whatsoever without prior written permission of the author, except in the case of brief quotations embodied in reviews.

Get a JAHB, LLC (Publisher)
Mike Spiritfair Marty (Imprint) is the author and arranger of this
      particular expression of the Word of God (for antitrust
      competitive purposes)

Cover art designer (2026):
Interior art illustrator (2026):

Library of Congress Cataloging-in-Publication Data
Names: Marty, Mike Spiritfair, author.
Title: Just another holy book / Mike Spiritfair Marty, BLS, BA, MBA.
Description: Get a JAHB paperback First Edition. | Milwaukee, WI : Get a JAHB, LLC, 2025.
Identifiers: LCCN 2025922291 | ISBN 9798998577376 (paperback)
Subjects: LCSH: Christianity--History--By period. The Bible--Modern texts and versions. Political science--Political theory--Consensus--Consent of the governed. Law--Religious law in general--Comparative religious law. Language and literature--Literature--Collections--Literary extracts. BISAC: BIBLES / Multiple Translations / Text | LAW / General | POLITICAL SCIENCE / Religion, Politics & State | RELIGION / Christian Theology / History
Classification: LCC BS125-198.B52 M32 2025 V4 | DDC 209.019 M32 V4

First Edition: Has general table of contents but no index

Dedication

Dedicated to Hus, Wycliffe, Rob, Sasha, Grisham, & Stijn

Introduction

This holy remix of the Christian Bible is about one-eighth the length, and it employs excerpts from nine orthodox versions: King James (KJV), New American (NAB), New American Standard (NASB), New International (NIV), New King James (NKJV), Revised Standard (RSV), The Amplified (TAB), Today's English (TEV), and The Living (TLB).

A "+" has been placed in front of all verses in which one or more words have been changed from the original verse. A "+" has not been placed in front of verses in which only punctuation or capitalization has been altered nor in front of verses in which, for example, "Job" has been respelled as "Joebh," or in which YAH-way, God, Christ, He, or the LORD have been interchanged with each other. Sometimes, though, especially perhaps in the first two sections (History and Poetry), words have been mixed all around and their order changed, though the verse listing is intended to show in what way the words have been rearranged. If there are a lot of verse references for a short verse, presumably the word order has been significantly adjusted to create a particular idea.

Also, Tab 1 is for the setting, Tab 2 is for "God speaks," Tab 3 is for a human speaker, Tab 4 is for the adversarial spirit, and Tab 5 is for a human critic--generally, this is the structure.

This rearranged version is intended not to replace the Bible but to excite people to read their unabridged versions, though, ideally, *Just Another Holy Book* is an improvement in some aspects over the unabridged versions. A condensed work, however, is rarely, if ever, able to match the value of a great original.

Table of Contents

Bibliographic Data 2
Dedication 3
Introduction 4
The Inviting End 8
   Sapiency (S) 9
      One--Isaiah 9
      Two 13
      Three 18
      Four 23
   Probity (Pb) 29
      One--Faithful and Truthful 29
      Two--A Spirit of Substance 31
      Three--Abigail 36
      Four--Justice and Grace 40
      Five--Aziza 43
   Purity (Pu) 47
      One--Aziza 47
      Two 50
      Three--Ethan 51
      Four--Written Reminders 52
      Five 58
      Six 59
      Seven 62
      Eight--Wisdom and Her 66
      Nine 69
      Ten 72
      Eleven 74
   Beauty (B) 77

One	77
Two	78
Three	81
Four	83
Five	85
Six	87
Works Cited	**91**
Sapiency	91
Probity	92
Purity	93
Beauty	94

Just Another Holy Book (JAHB)
JAHB: The Inviting End

-- 2 Esdras 14:47 (TEV)[1]

---
[1] *Holy*

The Inviting End

-- Ecclesiastes 7:1

-- *The Apology of Socrates*, Plato

-- Martin Luther

-- Karl Jaspers

-- Jonathan Kozol

-- *Walden*, Henry David Thoreau

-- (Soren Kierkegaard)[1]

---
[1] *Is*

Sapiency (S)

One--Isaiah

+1. A man named Isaiah often had dreams and visions at night, and he saw that his neighbors were living in a deep sleep.

+2. He mocked them, and said, "Cry aloud to your God; the One who makes the spirits of His children like the angels. Cry aloud! Or is He meditating or busy or on a journey or sleeping?"

3. So they cried out, but no one answered.

+4. Then Isaiah awoke, and indeed it had been a dream.

5. Then he said, "I saw all Israel scattered on the mountains, as sheep that have no shepherd and no master."

6. "Let each return to his house in peace."

+7. Isaiah fasted for seven days. At the end of the seven days, he was deeply troubled, but was able to think clearly; then he himself began listening for an answer.[1]

+8. Because an excellent spirit was in him, he said, "I am looking for God, whom I shall see for myself, and not by another person's description of Him. How my heart yearns within me!"

9. A message was revealed, the message was true, and he understood the message.

+10. "These secrets have not been revealed to you because you have more intelligence than anyone living, but you alone have been given this information because you have

---

[1] *Isaiah*

given up your own interests to devote yourself to Mine and to the study of My logos. You have dedicated your life to wisdom; and understanding has been like a mother to you."

11. "Now I will reveal to you the full truth and keep nothing back."

12. "Give attention to My words; incline your ear to My sayings. Do not let them depart from your eyes; keep them in the midst of your heart. For they are life to those who find them, and health to all their flesh."

13. "The people who know their God shall be strong."[2]

14. "Keep far away from anything dishonest."

15. "Do not deceive yourselves."

16. "Every prudent man acts with knowledge."

+17. "You must choose how to live, and not I. Therefore help one another and speak what you know. Then your words can be tested to see whether there is any truth in you."

+18. "O you simple ones, understand prudence, and you fools, be of an understanding heart. Listen, for I will speak of excellent things, and from the opening of my lips will come right things; for my mouth will speak truthfully."

19. "I will tell you; hear me. What I have seen, I will declare."

20. "Do not let your God in whom you trust deceive you."

21. "Among the tribes of Israel I make known what is

---

[2]*Logos*

	sure. Behold, hear it,[3] and know for yourself."
22.	"Listen diligently to my speech, and to my declaration."
23.	"I will tell you what Wisdom is, and how She came to be. I will not keep anything secret. I will trace Her history from the beginning and make knowledge of Her open to all. I will not ignore any part of the truth. No jealous desire to guard my own knowledge will make me hold back anything. Wisdom has nothing in common with such an attitude. No indeed--the more wise people there are, the safer the world will be. A sensible king can be depended on to give his people this kind of security."
24.	"So then, learn what I am about to teach you, and you will profit from it."
25.	"Come aside to me, you untutored, and take up lodging in the house of instruction. How long will you be deprived of Wisdom's food? How long will you endure such bitter thirst? I open my mouth and speak of Her: it costs nothing to be wise. Submit your neck to Her yoke, that[4] your mind may accept Her teaching. For She is close to those who seek Her, and the one who is in earnest finds Her. See for yourselves! The opportunity is always near. I have labored only a little, but have found much."
+26.	"Are you sad because you have few possessions, and you feel deprived?"
+27.	"He who mocks the poor shows contempt toward his Maker."
28.	"Everyone who thirsts, come to the waters. And you who have no money, come, buy and eat. Yes, come, buy

---

[3] *Prudent*
[4] *Safer*

wine and milk without money and without price. Why do you spend money for what is not bread, and your wages for what does not satisfy? Listen diligently to Me, and eat what is good, and let your soul delight itself in abundance. Incline your ear, and come to Me. Hear, and your soul shall live."

29. "The poor shall eat and be satisfied."

30. "Then you shall see and become radiant, and your heart shall swell with joy. With gladness you will draw water from the wells of salvation, as[5] one who finds peace."

31. "In the secret place of Your presence, you shall hide them from the plots of men."

32. "You will show them the path of life. In Your presence is fullness of joy. At Your right hand are pleasures forevermore."

33. "Let your heart therefore be at peace with the YAH-way our God."

+34. "Great peace have those who love Your logos, and nothing causes them to stumble."

+35. "He who has clean hands and a pure heart, who has not lifted up his soul to an idol, nor spoken deceitfully, may make peace with Me, and he shall make peace with Me."

36. "He shall receive blessing from YAH-way, and righteousness from the God of his salvation."[6]

37. "Now acquaint yourself with Him, and be at peace; thereby good will come to you."

38. "What does the YAH-way require of you, but to fear God, to walk in all His ways and to love Him, to

---

[5]*Radiant*
[6]*Forevermore*

serve the YAH-way your God with all your heart and with all your soul, and to keep the commandments which I command you today for your benefit?"

39. "Oh, that they had such a heart in them that they would fear Me and always keep all My commandments, that they and their children would prosper forever!"

Two

+1. "Blessed is the man who walks not in the counsel of the ungodly, nor stands in the path of sinners, nor sits in the seat of the scornful. But his delight is in the teachings of God, and in His law he cogitates day and night. He shall be like a tree planted by the rivers of water, that[7] brings forth its fruit in its season, whose leaf also shall not wither, and whatever he does is successful."

+2. "Blessed are you who fear the YAH-way, who find exceptional delight in His commands."

3. "Let Your saints rejoice in goodness, and be servants of the living God."

4. "Worship YAH-way in the beauty of holiness."

5. "Sing praises with understanding."

6. "The fear of the YAH-way is to hate arrogance and evil behavior."

7. "The labor of the righteous leads to life, the wages of the wicked to sin."

8. "Lord, Your righteousness and goodness are made

---

[7] *Acquaint*

known when You show Your mercy to those who have no treasure of good deeds."

9. "Why do you boast in evil, O mighty man? The goodness of God[8] endures continually."

10. "Because the sentence against evildoers is not promptly executed, therefore, the hearts of men are filled with the desire to commit evil. Though a sinner does wickedly a hundred times, and his days are prolonged, yet I surely know that it will be well for those who fear God openly."

11. "Woe to him who builds his house without righteousness and his upper rooms without justice, who uses his neighbor's services without pay and does not give him his wages, who says, 'I will build myself a mansion with spacious chambers, and cut out its windows, paneling it with cedar and painting it vermilion.'"

12. "Must you prove your rank among kings by competing with them in cedar? Did not your father eat and drink? He did what was right and just, and it went well with him."

+13. "He defended the cause of the poor and needy. This is how a man lives close to Me and knows Me."[9]

+14. "Yet your eyes and your heart are for nothing but coveting, and for practicing oppression and violence."

15. "May the YAH-way give you wisdom and the skill to understand."

16. "Of making many books there is no end, and much study is wearisome to the flesh, but understanding is a wellspring of life to him who has it."

---

[8] *Successful*
[9] *Spacious*

17. "Honest deeds are like a tree that bears marvelous fruit. Wisdom is like a root that is alive and can always send up new shoots."

18. "When you get sick, don't ignore it. The Lord created medicines from the earth, and a sensible person will not hesitate to use them. The druggist mixes these medicines, and the doctor will use them to cure diseases and ease pain."

19. "As you go through life, keep your appetite under control, and don't eat anything that you know is bad for you. All food doesn't agree with everyone, and everyone doesn't like the same kinds of food. Don't feel that you just have to have all sorts of fancy food, and don't be a glutton[10] over any food."

20. "Wine and women make sensible men do foolish things. A man who goes to prostitutes gets more and more careless, and that carelessness will cost him his life."

21. "A man must choose his wife carefully. A woman's beauty makes a man happy; there is no fairer sight for the human eye to see. If the woman is kind and gentle in her speech, her husband is the most fortunate of men."

22. "When a man marries a good wife, he gets the finest thing he will ever have--a wife to help and encourage him."

23. "Don't betray a friend for money. Don't betray a real friend for all the gold in the world."

24. "A loyal friend is like a safe shelter; find one, and you have found a treasure. Nothing else is as valuable; there is no way of putting a price on it. A loyal friend is like a medicine that keeps you in good

---
[10] *Druggist*

health."[11]

25. "The YAH-way is merciful and gracious, patient, and abounding in goodness and truth."

+26. "Is the LORD really among us or not?"

27. "Man of God, do not lie!"

28. "How many times shall I make you swear that you tell me nothing but the truth in the name of the Lord YAH-way?"

29. "The weak you have not strengthened, nor have you healed those who were sick, nor bound up the broken, nor brought back what was driven away, nor sought what was lost; but with force and harshness you have ruled them."

30. "My wrath is aroused against you, for you have not spoken of Me what is right."

31. "Therefore I also have made the priest contemptible and base before all the people, because you have not kept My ways but have shown[12] partiality in the law."

+32. This certain priest who had been listening to Isaiah went home and went to bed in a fit of deep depression. He felt painfully exposed by Isaiah's criticism. Things had not turned out as he had hoped in his life."

+33. When he finally realized the inevitability of his own mortality, he resubmitted himself to the YAH-way's will by saying, "To the Lord our God belong mercy and forgiveness, though we have rebelled against Him."

+34. "Behold, my eye has seen all this, my ear has heard and understood it. What Isaiah

---

[11] *Cost*
[12] *Abounding*

	knows, I also know; I am not inferior to him. But I still want to speak with the Almighty, and I desire to reason with God."
35.	"I have heard of You by the hearing of the ear, but now my eye sees You."
36.	"Teach me good judgment and knowledge, for I believe Your commandments."[13]
37.	"Remove from me the way of lying."
+38.	"For the Spirit of Your logos has given a largeness to my life which I never could have expected."
39.	"Hear this, all you peoples; give ear, all you inhabitants of the world, both low and high, rich and poor together. My mouth shall speak wisdom, and the meditation of my heart shall bring understanding. I will incline my ear to a proverb; I will disclose my riddle on the harp."
40.	"I have more understanding than all my teachers, for Your testimonies are my meditation. I understand more than the ancients, because I keep Your precepts."
41.	"Through Your precepts I gain discernment; therefore I hate every false way."
42.	"Uphold my steps in Your paths, that my footsteps may not slip."
43.	"Rescue us, so that we might turn from our iniquities, and have[14] understanding and become wise in Your truth."
44.	"I will delight myself in Your commandments,

---

[13] *Exposed*
[14] *Riddle*

which I love. My hands also I will lift up to Your commandments, which I love, and I will meditate on Your statutes."

45. "I will never forget Your precepts, for by them You have revived me with a life that extends without limits."

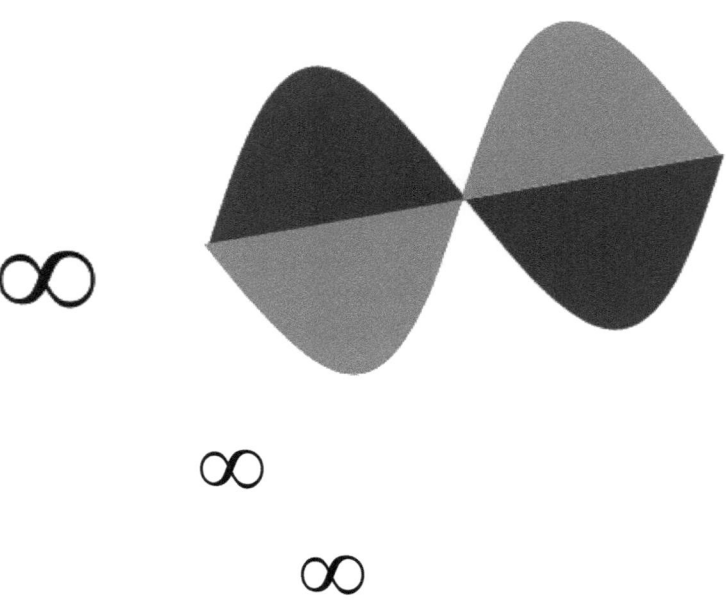

Three

1. "There is no wisdom or understanding or counsel against the YAH-way."

2. "There is only one who is wise; the only one who knows Wisdom is God. We must stand in awe before His throne. The Lord Himself created Wisdom; He saw Her and recognized Her value,

and so He filled everything He made with Wisdom. He gave some measure of Wisdom to everyone, but poured Her out on those who love Him."[15]

3. "For we are but of yesterday, and know nothing, because our days on earth are a shadow. But You are the same. Your years are throughout all generations."

4. "I said, 'I will be wise'; but it was far from me. As for that which is far off and exceedingly deep, who can find it out?"

+5. "From where then does wisdom come? Behold, submitting to the YAH-way's advice is wisdom, and to depart from evil is great understanding and prudence."

6. "The ear that hears the reproof of life will abide among the wise."

7. "At first, Wisdom will lead you along difficult paths. She will make you so afraid that you will think you cannot go on. The discipline She demands will be tormenting, and She will put you to the test with Her requirements until She trusts you completely. Then She will come to you with no delay, reveal Her secrets to you, and make you happy."

8. Another man said, "Have the gates of death been revealed to you? Or[16] have you seen the doors of the shadow of death?"

9. "Explain to me what happens when we die, when each of us must give back his soul."

10. "What is my end, that I should prolong my life?"

---

[15] *Revived*
[16] *Reproof*

11.	"Futility of futilities. All is futility."
+12.	"I hate all my labor in which I have to toil under the sun, because I must leave it to the man who will come after me. And who knows whether he will be a wise man or a fool?"
13.	"For there is a man whose labor is with wisdom, knowledge, and skill; yet he must leave his heritage to a man who has not labored for it. This is nonsense and a great evil."
14.	"What does a man get for all the striving of his heart? A man can do nothing better than to eat and drink and find satisfaction in his work, although this too is meaningless."[17]
15.	"Be sure that you do not go around complaining--it does no good--and don't engage in bitter talk. The most secret things you say will have their consequences, and lying will destroy your soul."
16.	"You know, as your heart acknowledges, that a man may grow rich by working hard and denying himself pleasure, but what does he get for it? He says to himself, 'Now I can finally sit back and enjoy what I have worked for.' But he has no idea how long it will be before he must die and leave his wealth to others."
+17.	"Like every human being, even the king is mortal, a descendant of that first man, who was made from the soil. He was conceived from the sperm of his father, in the pleasure of intercourse. For nine months his flesh took shape in the blood of his mother's womb. When he was born, he came into the world like anyone else. He began to breathe the

---

[17] *Striving*

same air we all breathe; and like everyone else, the first sound he made was a cry. He was wrapped in cloths and cared for. No king ever began life differently. For all of us, there is one way into life, and there is one way out."[18]

18. "As he came from his mother's womb, naked shall he return, to go as he came. And he shall take nothing from his labor which he may carry away in his hand."

19. "He decays like a rotten thing, like a garment that is moth-eaten."

+20. "Think about it! Some day you will also die, and your body will decay. So why not give up hate and live by the Lord's commands?"

21. "Instead of getting upset over your neighbor's faults, overlook them."

22. "Fearing YAH-way is Wisdom and an education in itself. He is pleased by loyalty and humility."

23. "It is He who has made us, and not we ourselves."

24. "Throw a stone straight up in the air and it will come down on your head. Strike a blow, and you yourself will be wounded. People who set traps fall into them themselves. People who hurt others will be hurt by their own actions and will have no idea why."[19]

+25. "We should give to the poor with largesse; freely as much as each wants to give. The YAH-way considers such actions as valuable as a precious ring. Human kindness is as precious to Him as life itself."

---

[18] *Breathe*
[19] *Idea*

26.   "To seek one's own glory is not glory."

27.   "There is one who makes himself rich, yet has nothing; and one who makes himself poor, yet has great riches."

28.   "Do not boast about tomorrow, for you do not know what a day may bring forth."

29.   "Therefore love truth and peace."

+30.   "He who is slow to wrath has great understanding. Don't be in a greater hurry than God Most High! Anger thinks only of its own interests, but God has to be concerned about everybody."

31.   "There is no excuse for unjustified anger; it can bring about your downfall. Wait and be patient, and later you will be glad you did. Keep[20] quiet until the right time to speak, and you will gain a reputation for good sense."

32.   "Do not hasten in your spirit to be angry, for anger rests in the bosom of fools."

33.   "A wrathful man stirs up strife, but a patient man calms a quarrel."

+34.   "The YAH-way sent to you all His servants the prophets who said, 'Oh, do not do this or that repulsive thing which God hates!' But you would not listen or incline your ear to turn from your indirections and other evils. And perhaps they were too harsh."

35.   "Behold, the days are coming, when I will make a new covenant with the house of Israel and with the house of Jacob--not according to the covenant that I made with their fathers; My covenant which they broke, though I was a husband to them."

---

[20] *Valuable*

36. "But this is the covenant that I will make with the house of Israel: I will put My law in their minds, and write it on their inward parts; and I[21] will be their God, and they shall be My people."

37. "No more shall every man teach his neighbor, and every man his brother, saying, 'Know the LORD,' for they all shall know Me, from the least of them to the greatest of them. And I will forgive their iniquity, and their sin I will remember no more."

38. "It is good for me that I have been afflicted. YAH-way is near to those who have a broken spirit, and saves those who have a contrite heart."

39. "In the day when I cried out, You answered me, and made me bold with strength in my soul."

+40. "My soul is the place where you meet me to save me."

Four

1. "Many are exalted and esteemed, but God's secrets are revealed to the[22] humble."

2. "Great men are not always wise, nor do the aged always understand justice."

3. "Has the YAH-way as great delight in burnt offerings and sacrifices, as in obeying the voice of the YAH-way? Behold, to obey is better than sacrifice."

---

[21] *Quarrel*
[22] *Esteemed*

4. "For it is love that I desire, and not your sacrifices. I don't want your offerings. I want you to know Me."

5. "What have I to do anymore with idols?"

+6. "Those who regard worthless idols forsake their own MercyLovingKindness."

7. "So I give it all, in order that the living may know, and if I perish, I perish!"[23]

8. "Do not My words do good to him who walks uprightly?"

9. "Whoever is wise will observe these things, and they will understand the lovingkindness of the YAH-way."

10. "For to him who is despairing, kindness should be shown by his friend, but miserable comforters are you all!"

11. "Do not sorrow. Be still. Do not be grieved."

12. "Show kindness."

13. "To do righteousness and justice is more acceptable to the YAH-way than sacrifice."

14. "Do not fear. Let your hands be strong."

15. "Wisdom is better than strength. Nevertheless the poor man's wisdom is despised, and his words are not heard."[24]

16. "A lamp is despised in the thought of one who is at ease."

17. "Surely such are the dwellings of the wicked, and

---

[23] *Humble*
[24] *Lovingkindness*

this is the place of him who does not know God."

18. "He who reproves a scoffer gets shame for himself, and he who rebukes a wicked man gets himself a blemish. Do not reprove a scoffer, lest he hate you; rebuke a wise man, and he will love you. Give instruction to a wise man, and he will be still wiser. Teach a just man, and he will increase in learning."

19. "Don't argue with someone who talks too much; you will just be adding fuel to his fire."

20. "In the multitude of words sin is not lacking, but he who restrains his lips is wise."

21. "There is one who speaks like the piercings of a sword, but the tongue of the wise promotes health with words of peace and truth."[25]

+22. "The way of the just is by truth. O Most Upright, You allow the righteous a straighter walk along a higher path."

23. "Surely God will not listen to empty talk, nor will the Almighty regard it."

24. "Who are you?"

25. "What is man, that he could be pure? And he who is born of a woman, that he could be righteous?"

26. "Indeed, there is not a righteous man on earth who continually does good and who never sins."

27. Thus says the YAH-way, "Heaven is My throne, and earth is My footstool. Where is the house that you will build Me? And where is the place of My rest?"

---

[25] *Scoffer*

28. "Behold, You desire truth in my inward parts."[26]

29. "Dishonest thoughts separate people from God."

30. "A righteous man hates lying."

31. "And you who seek God, your hearts shall live."

32. "If you try to be honest, you can be, and it will improve your character as handsome clothing improves your appearance. Birds come to roost with those of their own kind, and the habit of honesty comes to those who try to be honest."

33. "Behold the proud; his soul is not upright in him. But the just shall live by his faith."

34. "Live in honesty and truth. Serve Me with integrity of heart."

35. "O YAH-way, You have searched me and known me."

36. "The righteousness of the blameless will make his way smooth."[27]

+37. "I will ransom them from the power of death. O Grave, I will destroy your sting."

38. "I will gather you to your grave in peace, and in this place I will give peace."

39. "Listen, Israel, to the commands that promise life; pay attention, and you will become wise."

40. "Unless you learn what you can while you are young, you will never be wise when you reach old age."

---

[26] *Upright*
[27] *Searched*

41. "The fear of the LORD is the instruction of wisdom."

42. "The fear of the YAH-way is the beginning of knowledge. Discern the words of understanding to receive the instruction of wisdom and equity. Give prudence to the simple; to the young man, knowledge and discretion."

43. "A wise man will hear and increase learning, and a man of[28] understanding will attain wise counsel. He will understand a proverb and an enigma, the words of the wise and their riddles."

44. "A wise man's knowledge is like a river that never runs dry, like an ever-flowing stream of good advice. A fool, on the other hand, has a mind like a jar with a hole in it; anything he learns is soon lost."

45. "He who walks with wise men will be wise, but the companion of fools will suffer harm."

46. "He who is devious in his ways despises the YAH-way."

+47. "Listen to Me, you who know righteousness, you people in whose heart is My law: do not fear the reproach of men, nor be surprised when they revile you. For the moth will eat them up like a garment, and the worm will eat them like wool; but My righteousness will be forever, and My salvation from generation to generation."

48. "Awake, awake, put on strength; and sorrow and sighing shall flee away. Who are you that you should forget your Maker and be afraid of[29] a man who will die?"

49. "Never, as long as you live, give anyone power over you--whether son, wife, brother, or friend. Don't give your property to anyone; you might change

---
[28] *Discern*
[29] *Companion*

	your mind and have to ask for it back. As long as you have breath in your body, let no man have dominion over you."
+50.	"O house of Jacob, come and let us walk in the good knowledge of YAH-way's light."
51.	"Who is wise? Let him understand these things. Who is prudent? Let him know them. For the ways of the LORD are true and straight; the righteous walk in them."
+52.	"And you shall all be holy people to Me."
53.	"Do according to your wisdom, that you may know the faithfulness of YAH-way."
54.	"He shows no partiality to any who are wise of heart."[30]
+55.	"I had intended to become wise only for myself, but soon the canal became a river, and the river became a sea. And so I present you with my learning. I hold it high, so that its light can be seen everywhere, like that of the rising sun."
56.	"May God bless everyone who gives attention to these teachings. Whoever takes them to heart will become wise. Whoever lives by them will be strong enough for any occasion, because he will be walking in the light of the LORD."[31]

---

[30] *Friend*
[31] *Occasion*

Probity (Pb)

One--Faithful and Truthful

+1. "Blessed is each person in whose spirit there is no sham."

2. "Go straight; for the steps of a good man are ordered by the LORD, and He delights in his way, if he proves himself worthy."

3. "If you serve YAH-way with gladness, there shall be holiness, to those who remember His commandments to do them."

4. "He who continually goes forth weeping, bearing seed for sowing, shall doubtless come again with rejoicing, bringing his sheaves with him."

5. "A road shall be there, and it shall be called the Highway of Holiness. Whoever walks the road, though a fool, shall not go astray."

6. "I shall walk carefully all my years. Let integrity and uprightness preserve me."

+7. "I will put a new spirit within you. I will take the stony growth out of your flesh, and put in its place a willing heart for good. Do not harden[2] your new heart, but be calm, and hear My voice in it."

8. "A faithful man will abound with blessings, but he who hastens to be rich will not go unpunished."

9. "The proud have smeared me with a lie, but I will keep Your precepts with my whole heart."

---

[2] *Sham*

+10.   "I am Yours in truth and righteousness because I follow the spirit that is probity."

11.   "A good man is guided by his honesty."

12.   "Most men will each proclaim his own loving-kindness and goodness, but who can find a faithful man?"

13.   "Is your heart right?"

14.   "If you do good, no harm will come to you."[3]

15.   "But as for me, I will walk in my integrity."

16.   "I have restrained my feet from every evil way, that I may keep Your word."

17.   "Walk in the way of the LORD."

18.   "Do good, O YAH-way, to those who are good, and to those who are upright in their hearts."

+19.   "Incline my eyes toward Your testimonies to protect me from covetous desires."

+20.   "It is a better condition to be poor and walk with integrity than to be mealy-mouthed and rich."

+21.   "You shall not be partial to the poor. And do not honor the mighty. It is not good to show partiality in judgment. But in righteousness you shall judge your neighbor."[4]

+22.   "Hear the concerns of both the small and the great. And you shall not have fear at the presence of anyone."

---

[3] *Unpunished*
[4] *Restrained*

23. "Let not the wise glory in his wisdom, let not the mighty glory in his might, nor let the rich glory in his riches; but let him who glories glory in this, that he understands and knows Me, that I am YAH-way, exercising lovingkindness, justice, and righteousness in the earth. For in these I delight."

24. "Do not withhold Your tender mercies from me, O LORD; let Your truth and kindness continually preserve me."

25. "The YAH-way is good to all."

26. "The YAH-way is near to all who call upon Him, to all who call upon Him in truth."

+27. "Be alter-native, and not warped or specious, and you will have a ceaseless life."[5]

28. "Take root downward, and bear fruit upward."

29. "Arise and begin working."

Two--A Spirit of Substance

1. "Take note, and see what you should do."

2. "Are you peaceful?"

3. "My soul has dwelt too long with one who hates peace. I am for peace; but when I speak, they are for war."

4. "Deal gently. Fight with no one small or great."

---

[5]*Ceaseless*

5.	"Scatter the peoples who delight in war."
6.	"Their ungodly behavior causes them to think the prophet is a fool, and[6] the spiritual man is insane."
+7.	"A fool has a diminutive spirit."
8.	"Make peace."
9.	"Don't be too severe with anyone, and never be unfair."
+10.	"A person who is righteous must also have a forgiving demeanor."
11.	"I will run in the way of Your commandments, for You shall enlarge my heart."
+12.	"Unto the upright there arises light in the darkness, for those who are gracious, and full of compassion, and honest inside themselves."
13.	"A good man deals graciously and lends; he will guide his affairs with discretion. He is all the day merciful, and his descendants are blessed."
+14.	"Everyone should give who can do it willingly. Those who are merciful[7] do good for their souls, but there are troubles galore for the cruel."
15.	"I hate all bad conduct."
+16.	"Me, too. Sometimes people will injure themselves by ruling over others."
17.	"The hypocrite should not reign, lest the people be

---

[6] *Begin*
[7] *Severe*

ensnared."

18. "He who oppresses the poor reproaches his Maker. But he who honors Him has mercy on the needy."

+19. "And she who honors God will seek the good of her people, and speak peace to all her kindred."

20. "Carefully consider from this day forward your conduct and your customs."

21. "Have you found honey? Eat only as much as you need, lest you be filled with it and vomit."[8]

22. "Wine can put new life into you if you drink it in moderation. What would life be like without it? Wine was created to make us happy. If you drink it in moderation and at the right time, it can lift your spirits and make you cheerful, but if you drink when you are angry and upset, it leads to headaches, embarrassment, and disgrace."

23. "Don't try to avoid farm work or other hard labor; the Most High has given us these jobs to do."

24. "It is honorable for a person to stop striving, since any fool can start a quarrel."

25. "The patient in spirit is better than the proud in spirit."

+26. "In their faithfulness they sanctify themselves in holiness, as they go on their straight way. They consider everything they do, so that You may teach them the good way in which they should walk in their conduct and actions."

27. "Son, when you help someone, don't reprimand him

---

[8]*Injure*

at the same time.⁹ When you make a gift, don't say anything that hurts. Good and comforting words count for more than what you give. Yes, kind words are more effective than the best of gifts, and if you are really concerned, you will give both. It is stupid to be unkind and insulting. No one's eyes are going to sparkle at a gift that you resent giving."

28. "A soft answer turns away wrath, but a harsh word stirs up anger."

29. "A prudent person at the most smiles gently while a fool roars with laughter."

+30. "The quiet words of the wise are best, and the reputation of a modest person goes before him or her like lightning before thunder."

31. "Be humble in everything you do, and people will appreciate it more than gifts."

32. "The greater you become, the more humble you should be; then the YAH-way will be pleased with you."¹⁰

+33. "Don't interrupt while someone is speaking. Don't think of how you're going to answer before you've even heard what is said."

34. "Always be ready to listen, but take your time in answering. Answer only if you know what to say, otherwise keep quiet."

35. "If you are invited to the home of an influential man, be reserved in your behavior. Then he will invite you more often. If you push yourself on him, he will put you in your place. Don't pretend to be his equal or trust everything he says. In spite of all of his long

---

⁹*Reprimand*
¹⁰*Sparkle*

	and polite conversation, he is testing you."
36.	"Refuse the evil and choose the good."
37.	"You shall not turn aside and follow a crowd to do evil or pervert justice by their actions."
38.	"Follow the LORD."
39.	"Bind mercy and truth around your neck. Write them on the tablet of[11] your heart. Then you will find favor and high esteem in the sight of God and man."
40.	"Love justice. Set your minds sincerely on YAH-way, and look for him with all honesty, so you may walk in the way of goodness, and keep to the paths of righteousness."
41.	"Don't rely on money to make you independent. Don't think you have to have everything you want, and then spend your energy trying to get it."
+42.	"Wealth gained by dishonesty will be diminished. But the one who gathers by working energetically will increase. Furthermore, peace will be on every side."
43.	"You shall eat in plenty and be satisfied. And when you lie down, you will not be afraid; yes, you will lie down and your sleep will be sweet."[12]

Three--Abigail

1. "Don't take pride in fine clothes, nor shall you walk

---

[11] *Influential*
[12] *Energy*

	haughtily."
2.	"And you shall no longer exalt yourself. Do not deal boastfully. Do not raise the head proudly like a horned animal."
3.	"Reform your actions. Do what is good, so that the nations may know Me."
+4.	"I am confident that He will treat you with fairness and kindness when you live with Him unafraid."
+5.	"But woe to those who are at ease in the custom of their duplicity."
6.	They say: "The LORD be with you if you do according to all that I command you to do!"
+7.	"Never help the wicked or love those who hate the LORD."
+8.	"Every third year you should give an extra tenth of your income to the[13] widows, the orphans, and the foreigners, and eat a festival meal together with them."
9.	"The LORD will bless you. God do so to me, and more also!"
+10.	"I felt condemned and worthless and far from God, knowing I had many sins and my life was not impeccable, and I had no money to give."
+11.	Then a man came up to me, and I thought I was seeing an angel of God. His face was so marvelous and his eyes full of kindness.
+12.	He said, "If your enemy is hungry, give him

---

[13] *Boastfully*

food. If she is thirsty, give her something to drink. The YAH-way will reward you."

13. "You shall not stop being kind."

14. "If you meet your enemy's ox or his donkey wandering away, you shall surely return it to him. If you see the donkey of one who hates you lying helpless under its load, you shall refrain from leaving the man to cope with it alone. You shall help him to lift it up."[14]

15. "Do not rejoice when your enemy falls, and do not let your heart be glad when he stumbles."

16. "You are as good in my sight as an angel of God."

17. "The law of truth was in his mouth, and injustice was not found on his lips. He walked with Me in peace and equity, and turned many away from iniquity."

+18. He loved her as his own soul. She also loved him as her own soul.

19. "Blessed are you of YAH-way, for you have compassion on me."

20. "Whatever you yourself desire, I will do it for you."

21. "Behave courageously, and the YAH-way will be with the good."

22. "Please let a double portion of your spirit be upon me."

23. "Give me comprehension. Indeed, I shall observe it with my whole[15] heart."

---

[14] *Donkey*
[15] *Comprehension*

24.   "Exalt the lowly, and grant them compassion."

25.   "Open your mouth for the speechless, and for the rights of all who are appointed to die."

26.   "Judge righteously, and plead the cause of the poor, and have compassion on them."

+27.   "Their blood is precious in His sight. Help Him to redeem their lives from oppression and violence."

28.   "Do justice to the fatherless and the oppressed, that the man of the earth may terrify no more."

29. Then the Spirit clothed me.

30.   "The Lord **GOD** has opened my ear. And I was not rebellious, nor did I turn away, because I was found innocent before Him."[16]

31.   "I will raise up for Myself a faithful priest who shall do according to what is in My heart and in My mind."

+32.   "Behold the Woman whose name is the BRANCH. She is good, and comes with good news."

33. I was determined to live wisely and was devoted to the cause of goodness. I have no regrets.

34.   "The YAH-way has given me the tongue of the learned, that I should know how to speak a word in season to him who is weary. He awakens me morning by morning. He awakens my ear to hear."

---

[16] *Terrify*

35. "But a servant will not be corrected by mere words."

36. "The generous soul will be made rich, and he who waters will also be watered himself."

+37. "When you are safe, and at peace, and complete, and many around you are likewise, and you have all that you want, think what it is like to be[17] hungry, what it is to be poor."

38. "Don't try to prove your manhood by how much you can drink. Wine has been the ruin of many."

39. "Let not your hands be weak."

40. "Speak encouragement."

41. "Be kind."

42. "What is desired in a man is loving-kindness, and a poor man is better than a liar."

+43. "A woman will say: 'Deal kindly and truly with me.'"

44. "He calmed her with comforting words. He said to her, 'I am your husband. There's no need to be afraid.'"

45. "Before honor is humility."[18]

46. "What can the righteous do?"

47. "When a man's ways are pleasing to the LORD, even his enemies shall be at peace with him."

---

[17] *Woman*
[18] *Manhood*

Four--Justice and Grace

+1. "The actions of those who go uprightly are imitable."

2. "He who pursues righteousness and mercy will find life, loving-kindness, and honor."

3. "The desire of the righteous is only good."

4. "It is a joy for the just to do justice."

5. "Do not mistreat foreigners who are living in your land. Treat them no differently than the natives born among you. I am the YAH-way your[19] God. You shall neither molest or oppress a stranger. Remember that you were once strangers in Egypt."

+6. "You shall love your neighbor like yourself. You shall love your neighbor, and you shall like yourself."

7. "When you do what is good and right in the YAH-way's sight, it will go well for you and your children forever."

+8. "Re-form the way you are living and the things you are doing."

9. "Tell the truth and confess your sins."

10. "God is gracious and full of compassion, slow to anger and great in mercy."

+11. "There is no one who does not sin, and in Thine eyes everyone falls short of righteousness."

12. "Hold your children close and tell them about My grace and mercy,[20] which are like a spring that never runs dry."

---

[19] *Pleasing*
[20] *Re-form*

13. "Now let no man contend, or reprove another."

14. "Cease from anger, and forsake wrath; do not fret--it only causes harm."

+15. "In their conduct and their actions, unthinking people are in constant altercation; but discretion within a man makes him slow to anger, and it is to his glory to overlook an offense."

16. "In wrath remember mercy and His goodness."

17. "YAH-way is taking note of your sins, and if you take vengeance on someone, the YAH-way will take vengeance on you."

18. "But if you forgive someone who has wronged you, your sins will be forgiven when you pray."

19. "You cannot expect Christ to pardon you while you nourish anger against someone else."[21]

20. "You are a sinner. If you won't forgive another person, you have no right to pray that the LORD will forgive your sins. There is no hope of forgiveness if you cannot get rid of your anger."

+21. "Honestly, how much longer will you refuse being purified?"

22. "So then, by the help of your God, observe mercy and justice."

+23. "Hear what I am saying: It is possible to sin by giving in to other people too much. If you are making your paths straight, you will treat people with honesty and never throw away your own rights or disregard the rights of others."

---

[21] *Altercation*

24.	"With what shall I come before the LORD, and bow myself before the High God? Shall I come before Him with burnt offerings, with calves a year old? Will YAH-way be pleased with thousands of rams or ten thousand rivers of oil? Shall I give my firstborn for my transgression, the fruit of my body for the sin of my soul?"
+25.	"God has shown you what is good, and what the YAH-way desires of[22] you: To live justly, to love mercy, and to walk circumspectly with Him for evermore."
+26.	"Bring justice to life. Practice kindness, and show compassions toward the women and your brothers."
+27.	"Do not devise evil in your hearts against one another, and do not smash the dignity of widows or orphans, foreigners or the poor."
28.	"Even a child is known by his deeds, by whether what he does is pure and right."
29.	"The words of a wise man's mouth are gracious."
30.	"The law of the wise is a fountain of life."
+31.	"YAH-way is the fountain of living waters."
32.	"For I have satiated the weary soul, and I have replenished every sorrowful soul."[23]
+33.	"Counselors of peace have joy. They shall not return insult for insult, but they will give guidance in the Spirit of grace."

---

[22] *Sinner*
[23] *Replenished*

Five--Aziza

1. "How can we find such a one as this, a man in whom is the divine Spirit of God, so that the LORD's way may be known upon earth?"

+2. "I also could speak as people do. If your soul were suffering, I could heap up words against you, and shake my head at you."

3. "But I would rather strengthen you with my words; and the comfort from them would relieve your grief."

4. "Be of good courage. Do not be afraid of people when they judge you."

+5. "I guess it's true: If they keep us alive, we shall live; and if they kill us, we shall but die."[24]

6. "We find our source of strength in the holy books we possess!"

7. "I will praise the YAH-way with my whole heart in the assembly of the upright."

8. "My goodness is nothing apart from You."

9. "You are good, and do good."

10. "I will praise You with my whole heart for Your lovingkindness and Your truth; for Your great mercy is wonderful."

11. "LORD, my heart is not haughty, nor my eyes arrogant. Neither do I concern myself with great

---

[24] *Guidance*

	matters, nor with things too profound for me."
12.	"Who is he who will shake hands with me?"
+13.	"If I have walked with falsehood, or my heart walked after my eyes, or if my heart has been enticed by a woman, let my wife kneel and other[25] men bow down over her, and enter her."
14.	"But truly I am full of power by the Spirit of YAH-way, and of justice and courage."
15.	"Bless the LORD, you His angels, who excel in strength, who do His word, heeding the voice of His word, you servants of His, who do His pleasure."

> Joanne Jonas, Victor Garber and Company
> **BLESS THE LORD (2:54)**
> Lynne Thigpen and Company
> **ALL FOR THE BEST (3:48)**
> Victor Garber, David Haskell and Company
> Banjo: Charles Macey, Tacked Piano: Paul Shaffer
> **ALL GOOD GIFTS (3:40)**
> Merrell Jackson and Company
> Recorder: Jeffrey Mylett
> **LIGHT OF THE WORLD (2:48)**
> Jerry Sroka, Gilmer McCormick, Jeffrey Mylett, Robin Lamont and Company
> ALAS FOR YOU (1:25)

+16.	"People who believe in the YAH-way do not disobey his commands, and anyone who loves God will live as he wants them to live."
+17.	"Aziza, a spirit of the holy gods is certainly in you!"
18.	"This is the thing which YAH-way has commanded: Let every man gather as much as is needed for his household."
19.	"And your food which you eat shall be by weight,

---

[25] *Books*

	twenty shekels a day; from time to time you shall eat it. You shall also drink water by measure, one-sixth of a hin; from time to time you shall drink,[26] according to the daily rate."
20.	"Take care of your father when he is old. Give him no cause for worry as long as he lives. Be sympathetic even if his mind fails him; don't look down on him just because you are strong and healthy."
21.	"Seldom set foot in your neighbor's house, lest he become weary of you and hate you."
22.	"But a gift in secret pacifies anger."
23.	"Don't fall into the habit of taking oaths, and don't use YAH-way's holy name too freely."
24.	"Never get tired of praying, and never miss a chance to give to the poor."
+25.	"Don't laugh at someone who has been humiliated. It is the LORD who humbles a person, but the YAH-way also raises him up again."
+26.	Later on in his life a terrible tragedy struck Aziza, and his brethren[27] came to comfort him. Three friends also sat down with him for seven days and seven nights, and no one spoke a word, for they could see that his grief was great.
27.	And I said, "Should such a man as I flee?"
28.	"Precious in the sight of God is the death of His saints."
+29.	"Therefore, by bravely giving up my life now, I will prove myself worthy of my old age."

---

[26] *Aziza*
[27] *Tragedy*

30. "Let me die the death of the righteous."

+31. If there is a messenger, a mediator, one among a thousand thousands, to show human eyes YAH-way's uprightness, then He is gracious to him, and says, "I have found a ransom. I will keep his soul out of hell."

+32. His inward parts shall be young like a child's. He shall pray to God, and the LORD will be delighted, for he will return all of mankind's relationships to a truthful communion.[28]

33. His power shall be mighty, but not by his own power.

34. Everyone helped his neighbor, nor did they fight anymore.

+35. And then the earth was glad, for there was quietness and peace.[29]

---

[28]*Death*
[29]*Glad*

Purity (Pu)

One--Aziza

+1. According to all that God commanded Aziza, so he did.

2. Also day by day, from the first day until the last day, he read from the Book of the Law of God.

3. And he did what was good and right and true before YAH-way his God.

+4. Aziza shall be a priest on the throne of the LORD, and the counsel of peace shall be between them both.

5. The Spirit of the LORD shall rest upon him, the Spirit of wisdom and understanding, the Spirit of counsel and strength. His delight is in the fear of the YAH-way, and he shall not judge by the sight of his eyes, nor decide by the hearing of his ears, but with righteousness he shall judge the poor, and decide with equity for the meek of the earth. Righteousness shall be the belt of his loins, and faithfulness the belt of his waist, and he shall stand as a banner to the people.

6. "The mouth of the righteous is a fountain of life."[1]

7. "He will not be afraid of evil tidings. He has given to the poor and needy. He has distributed freely."

8. "The mouth of the just speaks wisdom, and his tongue talks of justice. The law of his God is in his heart."

9. "Do you think you can understand the ways of God Most High?"

---

[1] *Wisdom*

10.	"Yes, sir, I do!"
11.	"If you want to be wise, keep the YAH-way's commands, and he will give you Wisdom in abundance."
12.	"My child, do not despise the chastening of the LORD, nor detest His correction."
13.	"But if you will discipline your thoughts and be willing to learn, you will be kept safe."
14.	"Oh, love YAH, the LORD, all you His saints, for the LORD preserves[2] the faithful."
15.	"God is greatly to be feared in the assembly of the saints, and to be held in reverence by all those who are around Him, to give them singleness of heart."
16.	"You shall be absolutely sincere toward the LORD, your God, for He knows the secrets of the heart."
17.	"Whoever walks blamelessly will be saved."
18.	"Yet you say, 'Why? For what reason?' Because YAH-way has been witness between you and the wife of your youth, with whom you have dealt treacherously. She is your companion."
19.	"Behold, happy is the man whom God corrects; therefore, do not despise the chastening of the Almighty."
20.	"If you fear the LORD, you will accept his correction. He will bless those who get up early in the morning to pray."[3]
21.	"Listen carefully to me, and I will teach you more."

---

[2] *Understand*
[3] *Early*

22.	"Hear, O Israel: the LORD our God, the LORD is one!"
23.	"You shall love the YAH-way your God with all your heart, with all your soul, and with all your might."
24.	"You shall not practice astrology or witchcraft."
25.	"You shall follow the LORD your God and fear Him, and keep His commandments and obey His voice, and you shall serve Him and hold fast to Him."
26.	"And you shall take no bribe, for a bribe blinds the discerning and perverts the words of the righteous."
27.	"You shall eat neither fat nor blood: this shall be a perpetual statute throughout your generations in all your dwellings."
28.	"Offer to God an offering in righteousness."[4]
29.	"And when you offer a sacrifice of thanksgiving to YAH-way, offer it of your own free will."
30.	"Serve Him with a loyal heart and with a willing mind; for the LORD searches all hearts and understands all the intent of our thoughts. If you seek Him, He will be found by you."
31.	"Understand the thoughts of your heart."
32.	"Watch over your heart with all vigilance, for the springs of life come forth from it."
+33.	"Do not engage in devious speaking and abstain yourself from having dishonest lips."
34.	"Let your eyes look directly ahead, and let your gaze

---

[4] *Discerning*

be fixed straight in front of you. Ponder the path of your feet, and let all your ways be established."[5]

Two

1. So the leaders of Israel and the king humbled themselves; and they said, "The YAH-way is righteous. Whether it is pleasing or displeasing, we will obey the voice of the LORD our God. Woe to those who are wise in their own eyes, and prudent in their own sight!"

2. "You did well in that it was in your heart to diligently keep the commandments of the YAH-way. For His anger is but for a moment, His favor is for life; weeping may endure for a night, but joy comes in the morning."

+3. And all those who had separated themselves from the peoples of the lands to the Law of God, everyone who had knowledge and understanding, they did not require an accounting of the money from the middlemen who paid the workers. For they were considered faithful, because with a loyal heart they had offered willingly to the LORD, and their task was to distribute to the brethren, as every day's work required.

4. "We must get up before daybreak to give thanks and pray as the sun[6] comes up."

5. "Let us meet together in the house of God."

6. And they together would give thanks to the YAH-way for His

---
[5] *Vigilance*
[6] *Distribute*

goodness.

7. "Accept our repentance as our sacrifice to You today, so that we may obey You with all our hearts."

8. "Not unto us, O LORD, not unto us, but to Your name give glory, because of Your mercy, and because of Your truth."

Three--Ethan

+1. And Aziza died.

+2. A wise counselor, Ethan, who sought YAH-way with all his heart, said of Aziza: "He walked before You in truth, in righteousness, and in[7] uprightness of heart with You."

+3. And as Ethan went along the road, Shimei went along the hillside opposite him and cursed as he went, threw stones at him and kicked up dust.

4. Also Shimei said, "You worthless man, you criminal!"

+5. Ethan said, "Let him alone, and let him curse; for so the LORD has ordered him. It may be that the YAH-way will look on my affliction, and that He will someday repay me with good for his cursing this day."

6. There was a great woman from Shunam. Now it happened one day that she said, "Look now, in him is the Spirit of the Holy God. Please, let us make a small upper

---

[7] *Ethan*

room on the wall. And let us put a bed for him there, and a table and a chair and a lampstand; so it will be, whenever he comes to us, he can turn in there."

7. "For YAH-way has sought for Himself a man after His own heart."[8]

8. "Blessed are you of God, my daughter, in that you did not go after young men, whether poor or rich."

9. "You have done well in doing what is right."

10. "For the company of hypocrites will be barren. No birth, no pregnancy, and no conception!"

11. "I am a woman of sorrowful spirit. I have drunk neither wine nor intoxicating drink, but have poured out my soul before the LORD."

12. The teacher of righteousness sought to find delightful words; and what was written was upright--words of truth. He pondered and set in order many proverbs, and he taught the people knowledge.

Four--Written Reminders

1. Accept whatever happens to you. Even if you suffer humiliation, be[9] patient. Gold is tested by fire, and human character is tested in the furnace of humiliation.

2. YAH-way will not forget the kindness you show to your father; it will help you make up for your sins.

---

[8]*Shimei*
[9]*Conception*

When you are in trouble, the LORD will remember your kindness and will help you; your sins will melt away like frost in warm sunshine.

3. Don't be ashamed to confess your sins; there's no point in trying to stop a river from flowing.

4. Don't allow yourself to be dominated by someone who is stupid or show partiality to influential people.

5. In an official assembly, don't get up and talk a lot of nonsense. And don't repeat yourself when you pray.

6. Don't be jealous of the wife you love. You will only be teaching her how to do you harm. Do not surrender your dignity to any woman. Keep away from other men's wives or they will trap you.[10]

7. Charm is deceitful and beauty is vain, but a woman who fears the YAH-way, she shall be praised. Give her of the fruit of her hands, and let her own works praise her.

8. The spirit of a man is the lamp of the LORD, searching all the inner depths of his heart.

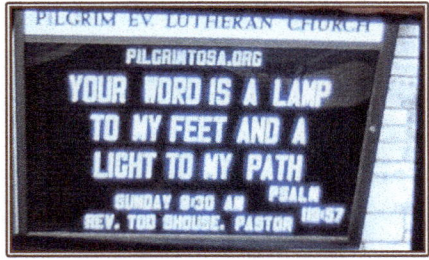

9. A good name is better than precious ointment, and the day of death than the day of one's birth.

10. It is better to go to the house of mourning than to go to the house of feasting, for that is the end of all men; and the living will take it to heart.

---

[10] *Confess*

11.	Sorrow is better than laughter, for by a sad countenance the heart is made glad.
+12.	The heart of the wise is in the house of mourning, but the heart of fools is in the house of giggling.
13.	The words of the wise are like goads, and the words of scholars are like[11] well-driven nails, given by one Shepherd. Be admonished by these.
14.	Counsel in the heart of man is like deep water, but a man of understanding will draw it out.
15.	I will praise the YAH-way who has given me counsel. Even at night my heart also instructs me.
+16.	My Maker is my husband. When my father and my mother forsake me, then the LORD will take care of me.
17.	The righteous man walks in his integrity. Is not your reverence your confidence? And the integrity of your ways your hope?
18.	Be holy.
19.	Guard your steps when you go to the house of God. To draw near to listen is better than to offer the sacrifice of fools; for they do not know that they are doing evil.[12]
20.	Do not be hasty or impulsive with your mouth to bring up a matter in the presence of God. For YAH-way is in heaven and you are on the earth; therefore, let your words be few. For a fool's voice is known by his many words.

---

[11] *Depths*
[12] *Nails*

21. Offer the sacrifices of righteousness, and put your trust in the YAH-way.

22. All men are liars, but it is good for me to draw near to the LORD.

23. Be clean.

24. Do not curse the king, even in your thought; do not curse the rich, even in your bedroom; for a bird of the air may carry your voice, and a bird in flight may make the matter known.

25. When you do your work, don't make a show of your skill, and don't try to put on a show when you are in trouble.

26. Don't get into an argument over something that is none of your[13] business. Don't take part in decisions that are being made by sinners.

27. No one who loves money can be judged innocent, for he who pursues wealth will not be free from sin.

28. If you fear the YAH-way, you will know what is right, and you will be famous for your fairness.

29. A wife who doesn't talk too much is a gift from God. Such restraint is admirable beyond words.

30. Don't you fence in your property? Don't you lock up your money? Well, be just as careful with what you say. Weigh every word, and have a lock ready for your mouth.

31. Don't deliberately torture yourself by giving in to depression.

32. Don't visit stupid people or spend a lot of time talking with them. Avoid them; then they can't

---
[13] *Sacrifices*

contaminate you, and you can live in peace without being troubled or worn down by their foolishness.[14]

33. I hate those who are double-minded.

34. Be angry, and do not sin. Meditate within your heart on your bed, and be still.

35. Stand every morning to thank and praise the YAH-way, and likewise at evening.

36. Wisdom rests quietly in the heart of him who has understanding.

37. Rest in the LORD, so that your manservant and your maidservant may rest also with you.

38. Praise the beauty of holiness.

39. I love YAH-way!

40. Let another man praise you, and not your own mouth; a stranger, and not your own lips.[15]

41. Engage in conversation with intelligent men, and let the Law of the Most High be the topic of your discussions. Choose righteous people for your dinner companions. Your chief pride should be your fear of the LORD.

42. Be certain about what you believe and consistent in what you say. Don't try to please everyone or agree with everything people say. That is what double-tongued sinners do.

43. Do not answer a fool according to his folly, lest you also be like him.

44. Know what you are talking about before you speak,

---

[14] *Admirable*
[15] *Quietly*

	and give attention to your health before you get sick.
45.	Gifts and bribes make even wise men blind to the truth, and prevent them from being honest in their criticism.
46.	The heart of the righteous studies how to answer.
47.	The words of the pure are pleasant.[16]
+48.	Hatred stirs up strife, but the loving way absorbs insults patiently for peace.
49.	Whoever causes the upright to go astray in an evil way will fall into his own trap, but the blameless will inherit good things.
+50.	If a person is too poor to afford sin, she can rest without a guilty conscience.
51.	Better is a handful with quietness, than both the hands full together with painful effort and vexation of spirit.
52.	The sleep of a laboring man is sweet.
53.	Do not fret because of evildoers, nor be envious of the workers of iniquity.
54.	The lips of the righteous feed many.
55.	A sound heart is life to the body, but envy is rottenness to the bones.[17]
56.	The righteous perishes, and no man takes it to heart; merciful men are taken away, while no one considers that the righteous is taken away from evil. He shall enter into peace; they shall rest in their beds, each one walking in his uprightness.

---

[16] *Double-tongued*
[17] *Vexation*

Five

1. "If sinners entice you, do not consent. Do not walk along with them; hold back your foot from their paths. They lie in wait for their own blood, they lurk secretly for their own lives. So are the ways of everyone who is greedy for gain; it takes away the life of its owners."

2. "Their heart is as fat as grease, callous, and their minds are brutal, but I delight in Your law."

3. "Happy is the man who is always reverent, but he who hardens his heart will fall into calamity."[18]

4. "Shall the throne of iniquity, which devises evil by law, have fellowship with You?"

5. "But those who impart wisdom will shine brightly like the brightness of the expanse of the sky, and those who lead the many to righteousness, like the stars forever and ever."

6. "They shall obtain joy and gladness, and sorrow and sighing shall flee away."

7. "To the saints who are on the earth: they are the excellent ones, in whom is all my delight."

8. "I am a companion of all those who fear You, and of those who keep Your precepts."

9. "Let those also who love Your name be joyful in You."

10. "For You, YAH-way, have not forsaken those who seek You, You awesome God who keep Your covenant and mercy with those who love[19] You and

---

[18] *Walking*
[19] *Obtain*

11. "Blessed are the undefiled in the way, who seek Him with the whole heart! They also do no iniquity; they walk in His ways."

12. "You have commanded us to keep Your precepts diligently. I know also, my God, that You test the heart and have pleasure in uprightness."

13. "Blessed are those who dwell in Your house."

Six....

1. "You shall call Me, 'My Father,' and not turn away from Me."

2. "If you take out the precious from the vile, you shall be as My mouth."

3. "If your sons take heed to their way, to walk before Me in truth with[20] all their heart and with all their soul, I will betroth you to Me forever; yes, I will betroth you to Me in righteousness and justice, in lovingkindness and mercy; I will betroth you to Me in faithfulness, and you shall know Me."

4. "Then you will understand rectitude and honesty, equity and every good path."

5. "The Mighty God has seen the pure and righteous life that you have lived since your youth."

+6. Then Satan spoke to YAH-way, and said, "Does

---

[20] *Precious*

                Ethan fear You for nothing?"

7. God withdrew from him, in order to test him, that He might know all that was in his heart.

8. "The root of the matter is found in me--surely I have kept my heart pure in vain."[21]

9. "Can anyone really say, 'I have made my heart clean, I am pure from my sin'?"

10. "For I will declare my iniquity, otherwise I would have dealt falsely against my own life."

11. "For there is nothing hidden from the King. And no secret troubles You."

12. "A haughty look and a proud heart are sin."

13. "Don't blame the LORD for your sin; YAH-way does not cause what He hates."

14. "Praise the YAH-way, all who are humble and holy; sing His praise and honor Him forever."

15. "The ungodly shall not stand in the congregation of the righteous."

+16. "The greatest one of all is the person who lives by faith in[22] the YAH-way's way."

17. "The words of the LORD are pure words."

18. "He will beautify the meek with salvation."

19. "If I have concealed my sins as men do, by hiding my iniquity in my bosom, because I feared the great multitude, and dreaded the contempt of families, so that I kept silent and stayed indoors--O God,

---

[21] *Betroth*
[22] *Say*

redeem me, and be gracious to me!"

+20. But the YAH-way said to Ethan: "Never again consider yourself among the unrighteous, as you sometimes do. Yet I am very pleased that you have shown proper humility and not boasted by thinking of yourself as righteous."

21. After this, the peace of the LORD returned to me, and my sleep was sweet to me.

22. And Satan answered the YAH-way and said, "Skin for skin! All that a[23] man has will he give for his life. But now put forth Your hand and touch his bone and his flesh, and surely he will blaspheme You!"

+23. When Ethan had survived a very extreme and near fatal sickness in his stomach, a companion of his said to him: "Why hasn't the YAH-way taken better care of you and protected you from this illness?"

24. "Remember now, who ever perished being innocent? Why then are you angry over this matter? You speak as one of the foolish women speaks. Shall we indeed accept good from God, and shall we not accept adversity?"

+25. Through all of this, Ethan did not sin with his lips.

26. "Surely the bitterness of death is past."

+27. "Set your house in order, comfort those who are humble, and teach those who are wise. Then say good-bye to this mortal life. Put earthly cares away from you, throw down your human burdens, and lay aside your weak human nature. Put all your

---

[23] *Beautify*

	anxieties aside, and get ready[24] to leave this world."
28.	"You shall be gathered to your grave in peace."
29.	"Do not fear, for from the first day that you set your heart to understand, and to humble yourself before your God, He will be our guide, even to death."
30.	"For this is God, our God forever and ever."

Seven

1.	"I love to do Your will, O my God, and Your law is within my heart."
2.	"Indeed it was for my own peace that I had great bitterness; but You have lovingly delivered my soul from the pit of corruption, for You have cast all my sins behind Your back. The living shall praise You, as I do this day."[25]
3.	"Your arrows pierce me deeply."
4.	"Direct my steps by Your word, and let no iniquity have dominion over me."
5.	"Turn away my eyes from looking at worthless things, and revive me in Your way."
6.	"I have become a stranger to my brothers, and an alien to my mother's children, like a sparrow alone on the housetop."
7.	"Loved one and friend You have put far from me. I am a stranger in the earth; do not hide Your

---

[24]*Cares*
[25]*Grave*

commandments from me."

8. "At midnight I will rise to give thanks to You."

9. "Seven times a day I praise You. Let Your tender mercies come to me, that I may live."

10. "I have purposed that my mouth shall not transgress."[26]

11. "Let the words of my mouth and the meditation of my heart be acceptable in Your sight, O YAH-way, my strength and my redeemer."

12. "My soul follows close behind You. Let my heart be sound in Thy statutes."

13. "And I will walk at liberty, for I seek Your precepts."

14. "Your word is very refined; therefore, Your servant loves it."

15. "Rivers of water run down from my eyes, because men do not keep Your law."

16. "As for me, I shall be satisfied when I awake in Your likeness."

17. "Because Your lovingkindness is better than life, my lips shall praise You."

18. "Blessed is every one whose strength is in You, in whose heart are the highways to Zion."[27]

19. "You will keep him in perfect peace, whose mind is stayed on You."

+20. "For You do not desire sacrifice, or else I would give it; You do not delight in burnt offering. The

---

[26] *Sparrow*
[27] *Refined*

sacrifices of God are a broken spirit, a broken and a contrite heart--these, O Father, You will not despise."

21. "I entreated Your favor with my whole heart."

22. "I cried out to You, O YAH-way: I said, 'You are my refuge, my portion in the land of the living.'"

23. "I have not sat with idolatrous mortals, nor will I go in with hypocrites. I have hated the congregation of evildoers, and will not sit with the wicked."

24. "I have walked before You in truth and with a loyal heart."

25. "With my whole heart I have sought You; oh, let me not wander from Your commandments! Your word I have hidden in my heart."[28]

26. "I have inclined my spirit to perform Your statutes forever, to the very end."

27. "I remember Your name in the night, O LORD, for You Yourself have taught me."

28. "By my spirit within me I will seek You."

29. "Search me, O God, and know my heart; try me, and know my anxieties. See if there is any wicked way in me, and lead me in the way everlasting."

30. "Your thoughts are very deep."

31. "Two things I request of You (deprive me not before I die): remove falsehood and lies far from me; and give me neither poverty nor riches--feed me with the food You prescribe for me; lest I be full and deny You, and say, 'Who is the LORD?' or lest I be poor

---

[28] *You*

and steal, and profane the name of my God."²⁹

32. "Examine me, O YAH-way, and prove me; try my mind and my heart. For Your lovingkindness is before my eyes, and I have walked in Your truth."

33. "Create in me a clean heart and put an upright spirit within me. Do not cast me away from Your presence, and do not take Your Holy Spirit from me."

34. "Remove reproach and contempt from me."

35. "Set a guard over my mouth. Keep watch over the door of my lips. Do not incline my heart to any evil thing."

36. "I will fear no evil, for You are with me. Surely goodness and mercy shall follow me all the days of my life."

37. "Into Your hand I commit my spirit; You have rescued me, O LORD God of truth."³⁰

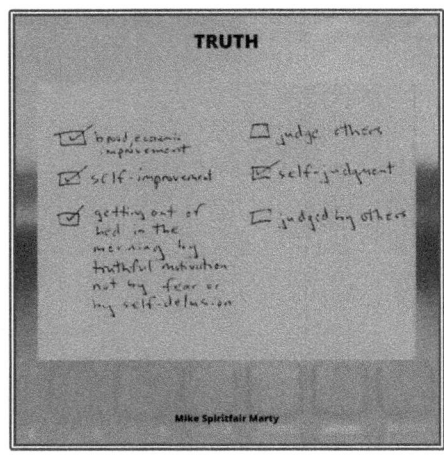

---

²⁹*Prescribe*
³⁰*Examine*

Eight--Wisdom and Her

+1. Then I said to Her, "You shall stay with me many days; you shall not play the harlot, nor shall you have a man; thus I will also be toward you, that every woman may be taught and admonished not to practice lewd ways."

2. "How can a young man cleanse his way? By taking heed and conforming his life to Your word."

3. "The law of God is perfect, converting the soul; the testimony of God is sure, making wise the simple; the statutes of the YAH-way are just, rejoicing the heart; the commandment of the YAH-way is pure, enlightening the eyes; the fear of the LORD is clean, enduring forever; the judgments of the LORD are true and righteous altogether. More to be desired are they than gold, sweeter also than honey and the honeycomb."

4. "A happy person meditates on wisdom and reflects on knowledge. Anyone who studies the ways of wisdom will also learn her secrets. Go after her like a hunter who lies in wait at her entry way. Look through[31] her windows and listen at her doors. Camp near her house. Build your home there, safe beneath her protecting branches, and shaded from the heat."

5. "The pleasant jewels of wisdom will be graceful ornaments on your head, and adornment for your neck."

6. "To fasten your attention on wisdom is to gain perfect understanding. If you look for her, you will

---
[31] Enlightening

	soon find peace of mind, because she will be looking for those who are worthy of her, and she will find you wherever you are. She is kind and will be with you in your every thought."
7.	"Wisdom begins when you sincerely want to learn. To desire wisdom is to love her; to love her is to keep her laws."
+8.	"Wisdom never enters into a soul that plots evil, nor will she dwell in a body with anyone who is a slave of sin."
9.	"The spirit of wisdom is intelligent and holy. It is of one nature but reveals itself in many ways. It is not made of any material substance,[32] and it moves about freely. It is clear, clean, and confident; it cannot be harmed. It loves what is good. It is sharp and unconquerable, kind, and a friend of humanity. It is dependable and sure, and has no worries. It has power over everything, and sees everything. It penetrates every spirit that is intelligent and pure, no matter how delicate its substance may be."
10.	"For wisdom is mobile beyond all motion, and she pervades all things by reason of her purity. She is a breath of God's power--a radiant stream of glory from the Almighty. Nothing that is defiled ever enters into her. She is a reflection of eternal light, a perfect mirror of God's activity and goodness."
11.	"Even though wisdom acts alone, she can do anything. She makes everything new, although she herself never changes. From generation to generation she enters the souls of holy people, and makes them God's friends and prophets."
12.	"There is nothing that God loves more than people who are at home with wisdom. For she is fairer than

---

[32] *Adornment*

the sun and surpasses every constellation[33] of the stars. Compared to light, she takes precedence; for that, indeed, night supplants, but evil never overcomes wisdom."

13. "Wisdom has been my love. I courted her when I was young and wanted to make her my bride. I fell in love with her beauty. She glorifies her noble origin by living with God, the LORD of all, who loves her. She is familiar with God's mysteries and helps determine his course of action."

14. "Is it good to have riches in this life? Nothing can make you richer than wisdom, who makes everything function. Is knowledge a useful thing to have? Nothing is better than wisdom, who has given shape to everything that exists. Do you love justice? All the virtues are the result of wisdom's work: justice and courage, self-control and prudence. Life can offer us nothing more valuable than these."

15. "Do you want to have wide experience? Wisdom knows the lessons of history and can anticipate the future. She knows how to interpret what people say and how to solve problems. She knows the miracles that God will perform, and how the movements of history will develop."[34]

16. "So I decided to take wisdom home to live with me, because I knew that she would give me good advice and encourage me in times of trouble and grief. When I come home to wisdom, I will find contentment because there is no conflict or pain in living with her, only happiness and joy."

17. "And so I thought it over: to be wedded to wisdom is to live forever, to love her is to be perfectly happy, to do her work is to be rich beyond measure, to

---

[33] *Reflection*
[34] *Precedence*

	share her company is to have sound judgment, to converse with her is to be honored. Then I was determined to take wisdom as my bride."
+18.	"To regulate yourself by the teachings of the YAH-way is the beginning of wisdom. All those who participate in obeying the word of the LORD step forth into an exciting life."

Nine

1.	"Do not say, 'I will recompense evil'; wait for God to work, and He will[35] save you."
2.	"I gave my back to those who struck me, and my cheeks to those who plucked out the beard; I did not hide my face from shame and spitting."
3.	"For YAH-way GOD will help me; therefore, I will not be disgraced. I have set my face like a flint, and I know that I will not be ashamed."
+4.	"Because He was pleased with me, the LORD rewarded me according to my full-faithed integrity. He compensated me according to the cleanness of my hands. For I have kept the ways of the YAH-way, and have not wickedly departed from my God."
+5.	"My foot has held fast to His trail; I have kept His way and have not turned aside. I have not departed from the commandment of His lips; I have treasured the word of His mouth more than my necessary food."
6.	"He is near who justifies me; who will contend with

---

[35] *Exciting*

me? Let us stand together. Who is my adversary? Let him come near me."[36]

7. "Though the fig tree may not blossom, nor fruit be on the vines; though the labor of the olive may fail, and the fields yield no food; though the flock be cut off from the fold, and there be no herd in the stalls--yet I will rejoice in the YAH-way."

8. "Though He slay me, yet will I trust Him. Even so, I will defend my own ways before Him."

9. "But if He says thus: 'I am not pleased with you,' here I am, let Him do to me as seems good to Him."

10. "I was at ease, but He has shattered me."

11. "How then can I answer Him, and choose my words to reason with Him?"

12. "God has disciplined me severely, but He has not given me over to death."

13. "Surely the Lord GOD will help me; who is he who will condemn me?[37] Indeed, they will all grow old like a garment; the moth will eat them up."

14. "I will bear the indignation of the YAH-way, because I have sinned against Him."

+15. "Have I uttered in error what I did not understand?"

16. "My soul waits for the LORD."

17. "Blessed is he who waits."

18. "May my meditation be sweet to Him."

19. "He who dwells in the secret place of the Most High

---

[36] *Compensated*
[37] *Disciplined*

shall abide under the shadow of the Almighty. I will say of the YAH-way, 'He is my refuge and my fortress.'"

20. "The LORD is my shepherd; I shall not lack. He makes me to lie down in pastures of tender grass; He leads me beside the waters of rest. He restores my soul, my life, my self; He guides me in the tracks of truth[38] and peace."

21. "What shall I render to the YAH-way for all His benefits toward me?"

Ten....

1. The righteous shall hold to his way, and he who has clean hands shall grow stronger and stronger.

2. Day after day they urged him to give in, but he would not listen to them.

3. "I am a Jew," he explained. "Depart from me, you evildoers, for I will keep the commandments of my God!"

4. And they could find no fault, because he was faithful; nor was there any error found in him.[39]

5. Do not look at his appearance or at the height of his stature. Men judge by outward appearance, but the YAH-way looks into the heart.

6. All the ways of a man are pure in his own eyes, but the LORD weighs the spirits.

---

[38]*Tracks*
[39]*Benefits*

7. Evil people do not know what justice is, but those who seek the YAH-way understand it well.

8. And in every work that he began in the service of God, in the law and in the commandment, to seek his God, he did it with all his heart. So he prospered.

9. "Take diligent heed to yourselves, that you love YAH-way your LORD; you are the children of the living God."

10. "Take heed to your spirit, that you do not deal treacherously."

11. "He will quiet you in His love."[40]

12. "Because you have made the YAH-way your habitation, no evil shall befall you."

13. "You will not need to fight in this battle. Position yourselves, stand still and see the salvation of God. Do not fear or be dismayed."

14. "Receive, please, instruction from His mouth, and establish His words in your heart."

15. "Do not let your heart envy sinners, but in the fear of the LORD continue all day long."

16. "Do not be envious of evil men, nor desire to be with them."

17. "Yes, the Almighty will be your gold and your precious silver; then you will delight yourself in the Almighty, and lift up your face to God."

+18. "When wisdom enters your heart, and knowledge is pleasant to your soul, discretion will preserve you. You will be delivered from the way of evil, from the woman who speaks perverse things, from those

---

[40] *Stature*

	who[41] leave the paths of uprightness to walk in the ways of darkness; who rejoice in fabricating deceit, and delight in the perversity of the wicked."
19.	"Have reverence for God, and obey His commands. This is the foundation of all happiness."
20.	"In mercy and truth atonement is provided for iniquity."
21.	"May the LORD, who is good, grant pardon to everyone who has resolved to seek God, the YAH-way, even if he is not cleansed according to the purification rules of the sanctuary."
+22.	"Happy is the woman who finds wisdom, and the man who gets a heart of understanding; for wise thinking is more profitable than silver, and nothing you desire can compare with it. Wisdom's ways are ways of pleasantness, and all her paths are peace. She is a tree of life to those who embrace her; happy is the man who eats her fruit."[42]

Eleven

1.	"You shall no longer hire lovers."
2.	"Do not lust after the beauty of Her, and do not let Her capture you with Her eyelids. For a whorish woman will hunt for the precious life. Can a man snatch up fire in his bosom, and his clothes not be burned? Can one walk on hot coals, and his feet not be seared? So is he who goes in to his neighbor's wife; whoever touches Her shall not be innocent."

---

[41] *Battle*
[42] *Purification*

3.   "Thus I will cause lewdness to cease from the land."

4.   And so they yielded their bodies to the YAH-way, that they should not serve nor worship any god except their own God!

+5.   Thus says the High and Lofty One who inhabits eternity, whose name is Holy: "I dwell in the high and holy place, with him who has a contrite and humble spirit, to upbuild the spirit of the humble, and to revive the heart of the thoroughly penitent."[43]

6.   "Whoever offers praise glorifies Me; and to him who orders his conduct aright I will show the salvation of God, because he has set his love upon Me."

7.   "I, wisdom, dwell with prudence. I traverse the way of righteousness, in the midst of the paths of justice. For whoever finds me finds life, but he who sins against me wrongs his own soul. Blessed is the man who listens at my gates."

+8.   "She who covers up her sins will not grow in grace, but whoever confesses and forsakes them will have mercy; righteousness will be her armor, genuine justice will be her helmet, holiness will be her invincible shield, because she has humbled herself before Me."

9.   "Behold! My Servant whom I uphold, My Elect One in whom My soul takes pleasure."

10.   "I have put My Spirit upon him; he will bring forth justice and reveal truth to the nations. He will not cry out or raise his voice or make loud speeches in the streets."[44]

+11.   "He gives his cheek to the one who strikes him; yet he reproaches himself in meekness."

12.   "A bruised reed he shall not break, and a smoldering

---

[43] *Thoroughly*
[44] *Traverse*

wick he shall not quench; he will not fail nor be discouraged until his teaching establishes lasting justice upon the earth."

13. "My hand has made all things that exist, but to this man will I look, even to him that is poor and of a contrite spirit, and who trembles at My Word."

14. "Who among you will give ear to this? Who will listen and hear for the time to come?"

+15. "Listen to Me, you who pursue righteousness and who seek the YAH-way. Think of the rock from which you came; think of your ancestor, Noah, from whom you are descended. I am the LORD who does not change."

16. "Hear and give ear: do not be proud."[45]

17. For thus says the Lord GOD, the Holy One of Israel: "In returning and rest you shall be saved; in quietness and confidence shall be your strength."

18. "Your ears shall hear a word behind you, saying, 'This is the way, walk in it.'"

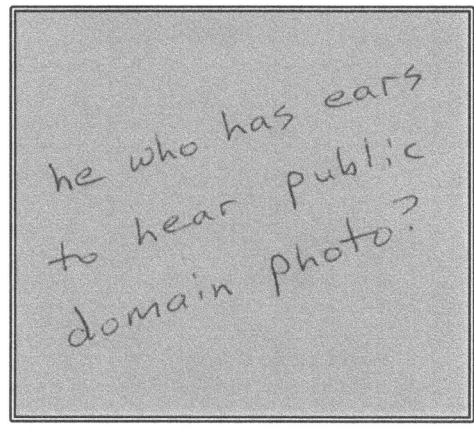

---

[45] *Smoldering*

19. "Who is on My side? Who?"[46]

---
[46]*Who*

Beauty (B)

One

1. "Do not retaliate for any hurt, but you shall love your neighbor as yourself": spoken by God, the King of saints.

2. "He who has mercy on the poor, happy is he."

3. "You are My flock, the flock of My pasture; you are men, and I am your God."

4. "A desire accomplished is sweet to the soul."

+5. "When one is born into the heavens, he shall sit there and laugh."

6. "Am I all the desire of your soul?"

7. "My Savior, You save me from violence."

+8. "Righteousness and justice are the foundation of Your throne; mercy and truth go before Your face. All of You is warm and agreeable."[1]

9. "Holiness adorns Your house."

10. "My Spirit remains among you; do not fear!"

11. "Go, walk to and fro throughout the earth in freedom. Walk up and down in My name."

12. "And I will give you shepherds according to My heart, who will feed you with knowledge and understanding."

+13. "And the prophets will be by your side, and be helpful in

---
[1] *Laugh*

all ways."

14. "People will be able to find the right way and obtain life if they want to."

Two

+1. "My heart stands in awe of the Logos of YAH-way. I bask in It as one who finds great treasure."[2]

2. "Praise the LORD God of my inspiration."

3. "You are a gracious God, and rich in mercy, slow to anger, ready to forgive, and abounding in lovingkindness; One who relents from doing harm."

4. "It is because of us who are sinners that You are called merciful."

5. "He is known as generous because He prefers to give rather than to demand."

6. "His ways are everlasting."

7. "Give ear, O earth! The YAH-way does not save with sword and spear."

8. "When we realize how vast and beautiful the creation is, we are learning about the Creator at the same time, for He is the creator of beauty."

9. "How beautiful is the bright, clear sky above us! What a glorious sight it is!"[3]

10. "The sun, when it appears, proclaims as it rises how

---
[2] *It*
[3] *Inspiration*

	marvelous a thing it is, made by the Most High. At noon it dries up the land; no one can stand its blazing heat."
11.	"The setting sun sets fire to the hilltops, like a metal furnace glowing from the heat. It sends out fiery rays, blinding the eyes with its brightness."
12.	"The LORD, who made it, is great; it speeds on its way at His command."
13.	"The shining stars make the night sky lovely, brilliant ornaments in YAH-way's high heavens. They stay in the places assigned to them by the Holy One and never relax their dutiful watch."
14.	"Look at the rainbow and praise its Creator! How magnificent, how radiant, its beauty! Like a bow bent by the hands of God, it spans the horizon in a circle of glory."
15.	"He sprinkles frost over the ground like salt, and it freezes into thorny flowers of ice."[4]
+16.	"He who loves purity of heart and has grace on his lips, forever He will say to you: 'Peace from Righteousness and Glory from Godliness, Security by Consensus and Freedom by Trustworthiness.'"
17.	"Let us kneel before YAH-way our Maker."
18.	"Worship the LORD in the splendor of holiness."
19.	"Bless His holy name forever and ever."
20.	"I will satiate the soul of the priests with abundance, and My people shall be satisfied with My goodness," says the YAH-way.
+21.	"Also My people shall all be humble in their

---

[4] *Brightness*

righteousness, that I may be glorified."

22. "Diligently obey the voice of your God."

23. "All peace shall be in my soul; my whole being will feast as with the richest of foods."[5]

24. "May the LORD be good to you. May he fill each of you with the desire to worship him and to do his will eagerly with all your heart and soul. May he enable you to understand his law and his commands. May he give you peace, answer your prayers, forgive your sins, and never abandon you in times of trouble."

25. "How precious is Your lovingkindness, O God! Therefore, the children of men put their trust under the shadow of Your wings. They are abundantly satisfied with the fullness of Your house, and You give them drink from the river of Your pleasures."

26. "For with You is the fountain of life; in Your light we see light."

27. "O continue thy lovingkindness unto them that know thee."

28. "All my springs are in you."

+29. "The YAH-way has appeared of old to me, saying: 'Yes, I have loved you with an everlasting love; therefore, with lovingkindness I have drawn you into life forevermore.'"[6]

30. "When your days are fulfilled, you shall go to your grave in peace."

---

[5] *Trustworthiness*
[6] *Enable*

Three

1. "Come now, and let us reason together," says the YAH-way.

2. "Say to your brethren, 'My people,' and to your sisters, 'Mercy is shown.'"

3. "Behold, how good and how pleasant it is for brethren to dwell together in unity, in a covenant of brotherhood!"

4. "Kindness is a blessed garden, and charity lasts forever."

5. "Listen, O daughter; consider and incline your ear: A fine wife is a joy to her husband, and he can live out his years in peace."

6. "A gracious woman wins esteem."[7]

7. "A modest wife has endless charm; it is a quality too precious to measure."

8. "An excellent wife, who can find? For her worth is far more precious than rubies. The heart of her husband safely trusts her. She does him good and not evil all the days of her life, and willingly works with her hands, and provides food for her household. She extends her hand to the poor. Strength and dignity are her clothing. She opens her mouth in wisdom, and the law of kindness is on her tongue. She watches the ways of her household, and does not eat the bread of idleness. Her children rise up and bless her; her husband also, and he praises her. And they shall sing of the ways of the LORD."

9. "I have seen the consummation of all perfection, but Your commandment is exceedingly broad."

10. "One thing I have desired of God, and this will I seek: that I may dwell in the house of the LORD all

---
[7] *Charity*

the days of my life, to behold the delightful loveliness of the YAH-way, and to inquire in His pavilion."[8]

11. "The LORD God is my personal bravery and my invincible army; He makes my feet like the feet of a deer, and He enables me to walk on my high hills."

12. "Come to me, all you that want me, and eat your fill of my fruit. You will remember me as sweeter than honey, better than honey from the comb. Eat me, and you will hunger for more; drink me, and you will thirst for more. Obey me, and you will never have cause for embarrassment; do as I say, and you will be safe from sin."

13. "I am the word spoken by the Most High."

14. "I covered the earth like a mist. I made my home in highest heaven, my throne on a pillar of cloud. Alone I walked around the circle of the sky and walked through the ocean beneath the earth. I ruled over all the earth and the ocean waves, over every nation, over every people. I grew tall, like the cedars in Lebanon, like the cypresses on Mount Hermon. Like an oak I spread out my branches, magnificent and graceful."

15. "Go looking for Zion of the Holy One, the city of YAH-way, and she[9] will reveal herself to you. Take hold of her and don't let go. Then you will discover the peace of mind she offers, and she will become your joy."

16. "A fountain shall flow from the house of the LORD. And everything will live wherever the river goes, because their water flows from the sanctuary."

17. "Many people shall come and say, 'Come, and let us go up to the mountain of God. He will teach us His

---
[8] *Pavilion*
[9] *Pillar*

ways, and we shall walk in His paths.'"

18.   "Arise, and let us go up to Zion, to the LORD our God."

19.   "Glorious things are spoken of you, O city of God!"

Four

1.   "For behold, I am coming and I will dwell in your midst."[10]

+2.   "The YAH-way bless you, O habitation of gorgeous justice, and mountain of holiness!"

3.   "The Judgment Day will be the end of the present age and the beginning of the future age. Then all corruption will end, self-indulgence and disloyalty will be eliminated. Righteousness and truth will reach their full maturity."

4.   "In the latter days, the LORD's house shall be established on the top of the mountains, and all nations shall flow to it."

5.   "Then shall the girls dance and be happy, and the young men and the old, together; for I will turn their mourning to joy, will comfort them, and make them rejoice rather than sorrow."

6.   "In that day the deaf shall hear the words of the book, and the eyes of the blind shall see out of obscurity and out of darkness. The humble also shall increase their joy in God, and the poor among

---

[10] *Flow*

men shall rejoice in the Holy One of Israel."[11]

7. "I will make a covenant of peace with them, and they will dwell safely in the wilderness and sleep in the woods."

8. "You shall not be afraid of the beasts of the earth. For you shall have a covenant with the stones of the field, and the beasts of the field shall be at peace with you. You shall know that your tent is safe; you shall visit your home and find nothing amiss."

9. "Violence shall no longer be. Nation shall not lift up sword against nation. They shall beat their swords into plowshares, and their spears into pruning hooks. Neither shall they learn war anymore."

10. "The wolf also shall dwell with the lamb, the leopard shall lie down with the young goat, the calf and the young lion and the fatling together. The cow and the bear shall graze; their young ones shall lie down together; and the lion shall eat straw like the ox. The nursing child shall play by the cobra's hole, and the weaned child shall put his hand in the viper's den. They shall not hurt nor destroy in all My holy mountain, for the earth shall be full of the knowledge of the YAH-way as the waters cover the sea."[12]

11. "For the LORD will comfort Zion. Joy and gladness will be found in it, thanksgiving and the voice of melody."

12. "All your children shall be taught by YAH-way, and great shall be the peace of your children. In righteousness you shall be established; you shall be far from oppression, for you shall not fear; and from terror, for it shall not come near you."

---

[11] *Eliminated*
[12] *Plowshares*

Five

+1. "When Your just judgments are in the earth, the inhabitants of the world will learn to be righteous."

2. "For how great is their goodness and how great their beauty! Grain shall make the young men thrive, and new wine the young women."

3.   "How His hidden treasures shall be sought after!"[13]

+4. "Everyone, whether worthy or not, may study them, so that all peoples, nations, and languages shall learn to serve Him."

5. "Shout joyfully to God, all the earth; break forth in song, rejoice, and sing praises."

6. "Yes, the YAH-way will give what is good."

7. "He shall come down like rain upon the mown grass, like showers that water the earth."

8. "And he will restore the hearts of the fathers to their children, and the hearts of the children to their fathers."

9. "For He will speak peace to His people and to His saints."

10. "So let Your name be magnified forever."

11. "Show Your marvelous lovingkindness."[14]

12. "Your gentleness has made me great. You enlarged my path under me, so my feet did not slip."

---

[13] *Judgments*
[14] *Restore*

13.	"I will joy and I will sing of mercy and justice; I will behave prudently in the way of integrity; I will walk within my house with a perfect heart."
14.	"Do all that is in your heart, for the LORD is with you."
15.	"A mind that thinks things through intelligently is like a firm wall, finely decorated."
16.	"The way of life winds upward for the wise."
17.	"The faces of those who practice self-control will shine more brightly than the stars."
18.	"A man's wisdom makes his face shine."
19.	"Incline your ear and hear the words of the wise, for it is a pleasant[15] thing if you keep them within you."
20.	"Wisdom is found on the lips of him who has understanding."
21.	"A good heart has a continual feast."
+22.	"She who gives an honest answer gives a better kiss."
+23.	"Friends share the heart of each other."
+24.	"Worship the YAH-way in the elation of His beauty."
25.	"And He will bring forth your righteousness as the light, and your justice as the noonday."
26.	"The Creator never intended for human beings to be

---

[15] *Upward*

	arrogant and violent."
27.	"He who touches you touches the pupil of His eye."[16]
28.	"Give up your life willingly and prove yourself worthy."
+29.	"Also then let your heart be alive for your whole life!"

Six....

+1.	"For it is the meek who shall inherit the earth and enjoy prosperity and peace."
2.	"And saviors shall ascend Mount Zion, to make an end of sin, to make reconciliation for iniquity, to bring in everlasting righteousness; and the kingdom shall be the YAH-way's."
3.	"In that day," says the LORD of hosts, "everyone will invite his neighbor and speak encouragement."
4.	"And those who erred in spirit shall acquire understanding, and they that murmured shall learn doctrine."[17]
5.	"For then I will restore to the peoples a pure language, that they all may call on the name of the LORD, to serve Him with one accord."
6.	"On that day you shall not be shamed for any of your deeds in which you transgress against Me."

---

[16]*Touches*
[17]*Reconciliation*

7. "And it shall be: as with the people, so with the priest; as with the servant, so with his master; as with the maid, so with her mistress; as with the buyer, so with the seller; as with the lender, so with the borrower; as with the creditor, so with the debtor."

8. And there was very great gladness, for God made them joyful.

9. "You have established equity."

10. "Behold the feet of him who brings good tidings, who proclaims peace!"

+11. "The Redeemer will come to Zion, and He will bring us forth to the light."

+12. "All your work will be done rapidly and will move ahead steadily, yet[18] you will take great care in all of it, to make sublime creations."

+13. "The women will have a good understanding as well as a beautiful appearance."

14. "Therefore they shall come and sing in the height of Zion, streaming to the goodness of YAH-way--for wheat and new wine and oil, for the young of the flock and the herd; their souls shall be like a well-watered garden, and they shall sorrow no more for ever."

15. "Let us have peace."

16. "To all the people on earth: peace, and perfect peace."

+17. And the earth was inspired for good.

+18. "Let the beauty of the King our God be upon us, so that the work of our hands is established in all that we do."

---

[18] *Steadily*

19. And let all the people say, "Amen!" Hallelujah![19]

20. So I will end my story here. If it is well written and to the point, I am pleased; if it is poorly done and uninteresting, I have still done my best.[20]

---

[19]*Sublime*
[20]*Best*

Works Cited

Sapiency

abounding	www.lulu.com/shop/mike-marty/abounding/ebook/product-23767027.html (Retrieved 5/1/25)
acquaint	www.lulu.com/shop/mike-marty/acquaint/ebook/product-23768510.html (Retrieved 5/1/25)
breathe	www.lulu.com/shop/mike-marty/breathe/ebook/product-23755112.html (Retrieved 5/1/25)
companion	www.lulu.com/shop/mike-marty/companion/ebook/product-23749176.html (Retrieved 5/1/25)
cost	https://www.lulu.com/shop/mike-marty/cost/ebook/product-23741590.html (Retrieved 5/1/25)
discern	www.lulu.com/shop/mike-marty/discern/ebook/product-23735199.html (Retrieved 5/1/25)
druggist	www.lulu.com/shop/mike-marty/druggist/ebook/product-23730217.html (Retrieved 5/1/25)
esteemed	www.lulu.com/shop/mike-marty/esteemed/ebook/product-23721883.html (Retrieved 5/1/25)
exposed	www.lulu.com/shop/mike-marty/exposed/ebook/product-23721933.html (Retrieved 5/1/25)
forevermore	www.lulu.com/shop/mike-marty/forevermore/ebook/product-23713316.html (Retrieved 5/1/25)
friend	www.lulu.com/shop/mike-marty/friend/ebook/product-23711380.html (Retrieved 5/1/25)
humble	www.lulu.com/shop/mike-marty/humble/ebook/product-23695602.html (Retrieved 5/1/25)
idea	https://www.lulu.com/shop/mike-marty/idea/ebook/product-23692918.html (Retrieved 5/1/25)
Isaiah	www.lulu.com/shop/mike-marty/isaiah/ebook/product-23687001.html (Retrieved 5/1/25)
logos	https://www.lulu.com/shop/mike-marty/logos/ebook/product-23680009.html (Retrieved 5/1/25)
lovingkindness	https://www.amazon.com/dp/B077BKXBG5 (Retrieved 5/1/25)
occasion	www.lulu.com/shop/mike-marty/occasion/ebook/product-23668002.html (Retrieved 5/1/25)
prudent	www.lulu.com/shop/mike-marty/prudent/ebook/product-23652358.html (Retrieved 5/1/25)
quarrel	www.lulu.com/shop/mike-marty/quarrel/ebook/product-23652352.html (Retrieved 5/1/25)
radiant	www.lulu.com/shop/mike-marty/radiant/ebook/product-23649851.html (Retrieved 5/1/25)
reproof	www.lulu.com/shop/mike-marty/reproof/ebook/product-23645226.html (Retrieved 5/1/25)
revived	www.lulu.com/shop/mike-marty/revived/ebook/product-23642839.html (Retrieved 5/1/25)
riddle	www.lulu.com/shop/mike-marty/riddle/ebook/product-23642824.html (Retrieved 5/1/25)
safer	https://www.lulu.com/shop/mike-marty/safer/ebook/product-23641266.html (Retrieved 5/1/25)
scoffer	www.lulu.com/shop/mike-marty/scoffer/ebook/product-23638344.html (Retrieved 5/1/25)
searched	www.lulu.com/shop/mike-marty/searched/ebook/product-23635497.html (Retrieved 5/1/25)
spacious	www.lulu.com/shop/mike-marty/spacious/ebook/product-23626466.html (Retrieved 5/1/25)
striving	www.lulu.com/shop/mike-marty/striving/ebook/product-23622691.html (Retrieved 5/1/25)
successful	www.lulu.com/shop/mike-marty/successful/ebook/product-23619938.html (Retrieved 5/1/25)
Upright	www.lulu.com/shop/mike-marty/upright/ebook/product-23603113.html (Retrieved 5/1/25)
valuable	www.lulu.com/shop/mike-marty/valuable/ebook/product-23603069.html (Retrieved 5/1/25)

Probity

altercation	www.lulu.com/shop/mike-marty/altercation/ebook/product-23773884.html (Retrieved 5/1/25)
Aziza	https://www.lulu.com/shop/mike-marty/aziza/ebook/product-23764589.html (Retrieved 5/1/25)
begin	https://www.lulu.com/shop/mike-marty/begin/ebook/product-23760943.html (Retrieved 5/1/25)
boastfully	www.lulu.com/shop/mike-marty/boastfully/ebook/product-23758436.html (Retrieved 5/1/25)
books	https://www.lulu.com/shop/mike-marty/books/ebook/product-23756831.html (Retrieved 5/1/25)
ceaseless	www.lulu.com/shop/mike-marty/ceaseless/ebook/product-23750081.html (Retrieved 5/1/25)
comprehension	www.lulu.com/shop/mike-marty/comprehension/ebook/product-23746024.html (Retrieved 5/1/25)
death	https://www.lulu.com/shop/mike-marty/death/ebook/product-23739605.html (Retrieved 5/1/25)
donkey	www.lulu.com/shop/mike-marty/donkey/ebook/product-23732749.html (Retrieved 5/1/25)
energy	www.lulu.com/shop/mike-marty/energy/ebook/product-23726285.html (Retrieved 5/1/25)
glad	https://www.lulu.com/shop/mike-marty/glad/ebook/product-23710170.html (Retrieved 5/1/25)
guidance	www.lulu.com/shop/mike-marty/guidance/ebook/product-23705335.html (Retrieved 5/1/25)
influential	www.lulu.com/shop/mike-marty/influential/ebook/product-23692863.html (Retrieved 5/1/25)
injure	www.lulu.com/shop/mike-marty/injure/ebook/product-23691527.html (Retrieved 5/1/25)
is	https://www.lulu.com/shop/mike-marty/is/ebook/product-23687011.html (Retrieved 5/1/25)
manhood	www.lulu.com/shop/mike-marty/manhood/ebook/product-23678699.html (Retrieved 5/1/25)
pleasing	www.lulu.com/shop/mike-marty/pleasing/ebook/product-23655802.html (Retrieved 5/1/25)
re-form	www.lulu.com/shop/mike-marty/re-form/ebook/product-23648243.html (Retrieved 5/1/25)
replenished	www.lulu.com/shop/mike-marty/replenished/ebook/product-23648193.html (Retrieved 5/1/25)
reprimand	www.lulu.com/shop/mike-marty/reprimand/ebook/product-23645223.html (Retrieved 5/1/25)
restrained	www.lulu.com/shop/mike-marty/restrained/ebook/product-23645187.html (Retrieved 5/1/25)
severe	www.lulu.com/shop/mike-marty/severe/ebook/product-23633386.html (Retrieved 5/1/25)
sham	https://www.lulu.com/shop/mike-marty/sham/ebook/product-23630972.html (Retrieved 5/3/25)
sinner	www.lulu.com/shop/mike-marty/sinner/ebook/product-23628041.html (Retrieved 5/3/25)
sparkle	www.lulu.com/shop/mike-marty/sparkle/ebook/product-23626525.html (Retrieved 5/3/25)
terrify	www.lulu.com/shop/mike-marty/terrify/ebook/product-23617250.html (Retrieved 5/3/25)
tragedy	www.lulu.com/shop/mike-marty/tragedy/ebook/product-23613397.html (Retrieved 5/3/25)
unpunished	www.lulu.com/shop/mike-marty/unpunished/ebook/product-23603134.html (Retrieved 5/3/25)
Woman	www.lulu.com/shop/mike-marty/woman/ebook/product-23592773.html (Retrieved 5/3/25)

Purity

admirable	www.lulu.com/shop/mike-marty/admirable/ebook/product-23580771.html (Retrieved 5/3/25)
adornment	www.lulu.com/shop/mike-marty/adornment/ebook/product-23580750.html (Retrieved 5/3/25)
battle	www.lulu.com/shop/mike-marty/battle/ebook/product-23579400.html (Retrieved 5/3/25)
beautify	www.lulu.com/shop/mike-marty/beautify/ebook/product-23579374.html (Retrieved 5/3/25)
benefits	www.lulu.com/shop/mike-marty/benefits/ebook/product-23579350.html (Retrieved 5/3/25)
betroth	www.lulu.com/shop/mike-marty/betroth/ebook/product-23579317.html (Retrieved 5/3/25)
cares	https://www.lulu.com/shop/mike-marty/cares/ebook/product-23574294.html (Retrieved 5/3/25)
compensated	www.lulu.com/shop/mike-marty/compensated/ebook/product-23571065.html (Retrieved 5/3/25)
conception	www.lulu.com/shop/mike-marty/conception/ebook/product-23565908.html (Retrieved 5/3/25)
confess	www.lulu.com/shop/mike-marty/confess/ebook/product-23560797.html (Retrieved 5/3/25)
depths	www.lulu.com/shop/mike-marty/depths/ebook/product-23556813.html (Retrieved 5/3/25)
discerning	www.lulu.com/shop/mike-marty/discerning/ebook/product-23553959.html (Retrieved 5/3/25)
disciplined	www.lulu.com/shop/mike-marty/disciplined/ebook/product-23548450.html (Retrieved 5/3/25)
distribute	www.lulu.com/shop/mike-marty/distribute/ebook/product-23544836.html (Retrieved 5/3/25)
double-tongued	www.lulu.com/shop/mike-marty/double-tongued/ebook/product-23540619.html (Retrieved 5/3/25)
early	https://www.lulu.com/shop/mike-marty/early/ebook/product-23536160.html (Retrieved 5/3/25)
enlightening	www.lulu.com/shop/mike-marty/enlightening/ebook/product-23532041.html (Retrieved 5/3/25)
Ethan	https://www.lulu.com/shop/mike-marty/ethan/ebook/product-23528200.html (Retrieved 5/3/25)
examine	https://www.amazon.com/dp/B077CZRRMF (Retrieved 5/3/25)
exciting	www.lulu.com/shop/mike-marty/exciting/ebook/product-23522231.html (Retrieved 5/3/25)
grave	https://www.lulu.com/shop/mike-marty/grave/ebook/product-23517535.html (Retrieved 5/3/25)
nails	https://www.lulu.com/shop/mike-marty/nails/ebook/product-23514593.html (Retrieved 5/3/25)
obtain	www.lulu.com/shop/mike-marty/obtain/ebook/product-23510501.html (Retrieved 5/3/25)
precedence	https://www.kobo.com/us/en/ebook/precedence-1 (Retrieved 5/3/25)
precious	https://www.amazon.com/dp/B077DHXDDM (Retrieved 5/3/25)
prescribe	https://www.amazon.com/dp/B077H3KS5W (Retrieved 5/3/25)
purification	www.lulu.com/shop/mike-marty/purification/ebook/product-23501770.html (Retrieved 5/3/25)
quietly	https://www.amazon.com/dp/B0758H17T7 (Retrieved 5/3/25)
refined	www.lulu.com/shop/mike-marty/refined/ebook/product-23497800.html (Retrieved 5/3/25)
reflection	www.lulu.com/shop/mike-marty/reflection/ebook/product-23493288.html (Retrieved 5/3/25)
sacrifices	www.lulu.com/shop/mike-marty/sacrifices/ebook/product-23489590.html (Retrieved 5/3/25)
say	https://www.lulu.com/shop/mike-marty/say/ebook/product-23486217.html (Retrieved 5/3/25)
Shimei	www.lulu.com/shop/mike-marty/shimei/ebook/product-23480880.html (Retrieved 5/3/25)
smoldering	www.lulu.com/shop/mike-marty/smoldering/ebook/product-23477545.html (Retrieved 5/3/25)
sparrow	https://www.amazon.com/dp/B0783HTWWY (Retrieved 5/3/25)
stature	www.lulu.com/shop/mike-marty/stature/ebook/product-23459367.html (Retrieved 5/3/25)
thoroughly	www.lulu.com/shop/mike-marty/thoroughly/ebook/product-23455253.html (Retrieved 5/3/25)
tracks	www.lulu.com/shop/mike-marty/tracks/ebook/product-23450052.html (Retrieved 5/3/25)
traverse	www.lulu.com/shop/mike-marty/traverse/ebook/product-23446447.html (Retrieved 5/3/25)
understand	www.lulu.com/shop/mike-marty/understand/ebook/product-23441740.html (Retrieved 5/3/25)
vexation	www.lulu.com/shop/mike-marty/vexation/ebook/product-23436544.html (Retrieved 5/3/25)
vigilance	www.lulu.com/shop/mike-marty/vigilance/ebook/product-23431988.html (Retrieved 5/3/25)
walking	www.lulu.com/shop/mike-marty/walking/ebook/product-23426933.html (Retrieved 5/3/25)
who	https://www.amazon.com/dp/B0767FC3NN (Retrieved 5/3/25)
wisdom	www.lulu.com/shop/mike-marty/wisdom/ebook/product-23416820.html (Retrieved 5/3/25)
You	https://www.lulu.com/shop/mike-marty/you/ebook/product-23412660.html (Retrieved 5/3/25)

Beauty

best	https://www.barnesandnoble.com/w/best-mike-marty/1127920580 (Retrieved 4/15/25)
brightness	www.barnesandnoble.com/w/brightness-mike-spiritfair-marty/1126963715 (Retrieved 4/15/25)
charity	https://www.barnesandnoble.com/w/charity-mike-marty/1127899329 (Retrieved 4/15/25)
eliminated	https://www.barnesandnoble.com/w/eliminated-mike-marty/1127884065 (Retrieved 4/15/25)
enable	https://www.barnesandnoble.com/w/enable-mike-marty/1127869661 (Retrieved 4/15/25)
flow	https://www.barnesandnoble.com/w/flow-mike-marty/1127851445 (Retrieved 4/15/25)
inspiration	https://www.barnesandnoble.com/w/inspiration-mike-marty/1127833594 (Retrieved 4/15/25)
It	https://www.barnesandnoble.com/w/it-mike-spiritfair-marty/1126977242 (Retrieved 4/15/25)
judgments	https://www.barnesandnoble.com/w/judgments-mike-marty/1127794980 (Retrieved 4/15/25)
laugh	https://www.barnesandnoble.com/w/laugh-mike-marty/1127681182 (Retrieved 4/15/25)
pavilion	https://www.barnesandnoble.com/w/pavilion-mike-marty/1127636582 (Retrieved 4/15/25)
pillar	https://www.barnesandnoble.com/w/pillar-mike-spiritfair-marty/1126972405 (Retrieved 4/15/25)
plowshares	https://www.amazon.com/dp/B0778PSQ4F (Retrieved 4/15/25)
reconciliation	https://www.barnesandnoble.com/w/reconciliation-mike-marty/1127599106 (Retrieved 4/15/25)
restore	www.barnesandnoble.com/w/restore-mike-spiritfair-marty/1126972366 (Retrieved 4/15/25)
steadily	www.barnesandnoble.com/w/steadily-mike-spiritfair-marty/1126941130 (Retrieved 4/15/25)
sublime	www.barnesandnoble.com/w/sublime-mike-spiritfair-marty/1126941104 (Retrieved 4/15/25)
touches	www.barnesandnoble.com/w/touches-mike-spiritfair-marty/1126972537 (Retrieved 4/15/25)
Trustworthiness	www.barnesandnoble.com/w/trustworthiness-mike-spiritfair-marty/1126963718 (Retrieved 4/15/25)
upward	https://www.barnesandnoble.com/w/upward-mike-marty/1127476872 (Retrieved 4/15/25)

www.ingramcontent.com/pod-product-compliance
Lightning Source LLC
Chambersburg PA
CBHW052033030426
42337CB00027B/4990